In Search of My Self

In Search of My Self

Basil Arbour

NOVALIS

In Search Of My Self is published by Novalis.

Cover: Robert Vienneau
Cover photo: Softkey PhotoDisk
Layout: Gilles Lepine

© 1996, Novalis

Business Office: Novalis
                   49 Front St. East, 2nd Floor
                   Toronto, Ontario
                   M5E 1B3
Editorial Office: Novalis
                   223 Main Street
                   Ottawa, Ontario
                   K1S 1C4

Printed in Canada.

Canadian Cataloguing in Publication Data

Arbour, Basil
        In search of my self

ISBN: 2-89088-753-7

    1. Devotional Literature   I. Title

BX2182.2A75 1995   242   C95-900741-5

For
Jean-Paul and Monique,
my children, my friends

All my students who have been
my teachers over the years

Jack Gear,
healer, counsellor, friend

My friends on the staff of
St. Thomas Aquinas High School, Oakville

Natasha Nunes, with thanks
for her story about the meaning of life

Contents

Prayer and Prayers

Other Scriptural Prayers

Significant Moments of Prayer

Exercises for Body, Mind and Spirit

A Parable

The following parable is essential to understanding why this book was written.

On a day much like this one, a pilgrim came in search of a holy man and posed the eternal question: "What is the meaning of life?"

Without a word, the old one took him by the arm and led him to a forest path. Encountering a snail on its leisurely journey, they stopped to observe its progress. After awhile, the old one left him alone.

But the very next day, the pilgrim returned and said: "I still do not have the answer to my question." And the holy man took him back along the path until they came to an expansive meadow. There he pointed to a bee, a badger and a butterfly, then left.

Again, the following morning, the young man returned, frustrated and confused. "I do not understand what you would have me understand."

The wise man smiled calmly and led him to a mountain pool, pointing to its waters before stepping back. The pilgrim looked down and saw in its depths the rock and soil which bind the earth. There could also be seen the energetic movement of the clouds through the heavens. Puzzled, he looked over his shoulder at the wise man, who simply pointed again to the pool's depth. Turning back to the waters, he noted for the first time his own reflection.

Peace and a great light filled his innermost self. He turned again, only to find the old one gone. But he was free.

Going back down the mountain trail, he greeted the snail which continued on its leisurely journey. And he returned to the meadow where he looked anew in wonder at the bee, the badger and the butterfly.

The Essential Human Task

Each of us has but one task in life. That task is to be discovered in the use of our individual gifts and talents. We are to become "holy" in the fullest sense of this word.

Everything we do and say is an attempt to assert the meaning of who we are and to become fulfilled in the process. If life is to be worthwhile and if we do not wish to encounter death with a whimper of despair, each of us must find *wholeness*. The wholeness to which we are called is the root meaning of the word *holy*. We are called to establish our connection to all life within the context of who we are – here and now. This discovery can have many names, but we most frequently call it "spirituality."

Most of our accepted spiritual practices come to us from a past where life was short and, for the most part, from attitudes that saw the world as a testing place for the life to come. Too often, the spiritual values handed down were to be found in either avoidance or withdrawal from what could distract us from the "real" purpose of living – the afterlife to come.

How many of us see the world in such a negative way? How many are able to live out the "monastic" vision? In reality, this world is God's. We cannot come to

3

a true understanding of who we are by refusing the challenges of living within the present moment. Again, this is God's *world*. It is not a test, but an experience by which we come to know our deepest self. We are part of this wonder-filled creation. It is "now" that we find genuine salvation; it is "here" that we work for the wholeness which leads to fullness of life.

Although the world presents us with many challenges – not the least of which relates to the good and evil we daily encounter – the primary challenge comes to us from the creative energy which is ultimately God. Life is basically good and offers us a multitude of ways to grow and change and find fulfilment. We are not locked into a cycle of time which we cannot alter.

Many have turned away, however, from a theology that speaks of the instincts of men and women as "bad." Many reject those things which turn us away from searching into our "here and now" and which prevent us from coming to know our individual self as connected to the whole of life. We must be aware that only through the "call" of others, and through the sacredness of life in the "now", is our deepest self realized.

Our response to the world is critical. And since it appears that each age is called to seek God within the grace given to that age, we are bound to look within our desires, hopes and dreams to create with God the full meaning of this particular moment. We are God's covenant partners. Any religious attitudes which deny newer and more far-reaching possibilities for human growth should be challenged. In fact, we should challenge anything which turns us away from the task of making this world a better place in which to live and grow. Heaven can – and will – wait!

We ought to view the world creatively, just as the Creator views it. No part can be rejected or ignored – even the darkness within our selves. God speaks to all dimensions of the human spirit. The Creator speaks within the wounded parts and within those parts where we find joy. And so we need to learn how to listen with our hearts as well as our ears; how to see with our spirits and our eyes. This imperfect world is given to us to shape and also to love through the wisdom of the One we name God. There is no understanding without the appreciation that everything is, and can be, redeemed.

My approach does not dismiss sin nor its effects on human life. Sin most often occurs because we are searching for meaning; we are still incomplete, still on our journey. But what becomes most obvious as we explore life with hope is that a lasting spirituality can be built only on the creative energy within each of us – risking, never avoiding situations where we might falter, fail or even sin. The power of our creativity is given and sustained by the Creator. It is God who calls us to a full life, and who forgives when we fail. Indeed, being human, all of us will inevitably experience failure.

What this world tells us, if we care to listen, is that we are all in this together. We need one another to realize our full human potential. No one can find "the answer" independent of positive, growing relationships. The exceptional athlete is known only in comparison to others. Those who excel are not superior, but find their potential in being connected with the talents of others. In the same way, I, the author, will have little or no success without you, the reader. We need each other to identify, challenge and discover common threads of experience.

As a Christian who finds in the ministry of Jesus a connection to the meaning of life, I dare say his life would have been incomplete without us – without someone to hear and say "yes" to his message. Heresy? I think not! This is simply the way that God has chosen to share his life within the context of time and space.

Whatever is of use in these pages is a gift. But beware! It is a gift to be taken with a grain of salt, the salt to be found within your own rich experience.

Build on whatever you find here. Remember, I am freed, but also limited by my own talents. I can only speak from the fragment of my own experience. You, too, are called to speak from yours.

And so we face the task together: to open the pages of the "book of life" wherein our names are inscribed. Make no mistake about it: good or bad, each of us will write a unique story about life and love and our journey in search of self. May God's grace fill us as we strive together with generosity and hope to enter fully into the dialogue of living.

How to Use This Book

This book is a series of conversations with God, with myself and with you. It includes reflections on my life's journey, stories, prayers and exercises which I have found enriching in the search for my self, for life's deepest meaning, for the Source and End to which all life is moving.

A cautionary note! There is no *one* way, especially in the spiritual life. As you search through your own joys, sorrows and questions, you will come to unique insights. You will come to prayer, which is the outpouring of the inner life in response to God, and which none can deny, save at the cost of the deepest self. Each person is like a snowflake – unique and unrepeatable. And so the prayer which flows from your own uniqueness will be very personal indeed, finding its own path until you come to understand your connection to all that God offers. Trust yourself!

You may experience difficulty if you limit yourself to traditional formulae and classical prayer. They can be good, but only if they lead you to *pray* – in other words, if they honour the movement of the spirit within. Only in this way will you learn to "listen" to the mysterious movement of your own life.

Much of what is and can become true prayer is to be found in the stillness of the heart. Here God can be heard most clearly. Whenever, for example, Jesus was preparing for the tasks of his ministry, he went into solitude. The desert was the first of such places. You, too, must go into your own desert, searching for release from the push and pull of daily activity, from the noise that distracts.

"If water reaches clarity in stillness, how much more the faculties of the mind." Those are the words of the Taoist master, Chuang-tzu. And God, speaking to us through the Psalmist, says: "Be still and know that I am God."

While reading these pages, you will find the outpouring of one heart, coloured by the warmth, the pain, the light and darkness of my own experience. Life, of course, does not always bring peace; fear and doubt are also vital dimensions. I have just begun to accept them all, finding in their diversity the movement of the Spirit. Through, behind, and under them all, I have come to see that I am connected not only to the Centre of Life – the one true God – but to all that touches me in creation at large.

Again: these words, stories, prayers and reflections are my own. You are invited to find your own way. Use whatever touches you in these pages, but also realize that, in the final analysis, you are called to create your own way of coming fully into your self.

Reflections

Talking with God

When we talk with God, it often seems that we are giving God instructions. We want God to do what we want or deem right. Indeed, this is often the stumbling block in developing the relationship. Besides, if God knows everything, then our needs and requests are already known. If life, moreover, has anything to teach us, it must be that God is beyond our control and instruction. The words, then, used for prayer must recognize this fact. The God who moves our hearts can only be reached when definitions cease. Listening opens us up to the movement of God's Life within and around us – a movement heard in and through people and events which touch our daily living.

No matter how great our efforts, we all reach that telling moment where we recognize the words written by the author of Sirach 43. The author's prayer became my prayer because the words address what I have just begun to know about God.

Though we speak many words
we cannot say all,
and the final end of our words is:
you are all.
Where can we find the strength
to truly praise you?
You are greater than all you have made.
Awesome are you, Lord,
and we marvel at your power.
When we praise you,
although we put forth our greatest effort,
this, too, you surpass.
When we proclaim you with our feeble efforts,
although many, still this is not enough.
Who is there who has seen you
and can speak to us of what you truly are?
Much of what you have done still lies hidden,
and we know so little of your greatness.
For you, Lord, have made all things,
and you have granted wisdom
to all those who come seeking you.

In most writings of the mystics, God is so described. Only when these holy men and women stopped speaking and writing, and gave themselves over to their deepest longings did they experience God's mystery, which moves beyond words.

This opening up of one's self to the mystery of God is not always attractive to those who want everything in nice neat packages. It is especially difficult for those who want an absolute, unshakable understanding of God. But scriptural commandments and theological formulae can never fully explain who God is; nor can they satisfy the human need to control. Instead, what the spiritual writers show us clearly is the sort of God who is full of surprises, who likes our questions and who is still in the process of creating life.

When I pray nowadays, it is in everyday words which arise from a multitude of sources: the stirrings of my heart, my deepening understanding of self, and from my relation to the God who speaks from the centre of creation. These words are centred in the daily encounters which both puzzle me and bring me joy. After all, prayer springs from those areas of life which twist the heart, leaving us content or perhaps even terrified. From these same moments, God is both known and yet remains mystery.

I have found that (even in this writing) God reaches out, giving me strength, allowing me to be more fully alive. Birth, death, pain and ecstasy – all are vehicles for the voice of God. Such experiences are the stuff of life, common to all, things we know but cannot fully grasp. Indeed, only when we are moved beyond our capacity to understand are we truly capable of prayer.

Most of us are better at speaking *about* God than we are at speaking *with* God. Even now, as I write these words, I am aware of my inadequacies at expressing my relationship to God and of understanding God's response. I still fill the space between God and me with too many words. And I have trouble sitting quietly so God can fill the space between us. Prayer, after all, is a two-way street. It requires much patience and courage to let God be God.

God is the great Presence, the great "I AM" of creation. Much of God's response will be in and through daily activities, through people, achievements, words of praise, hatred felt, failures, tears shed or wiped away, and all those other ins and outs of everyday life. This does not mean that God never speaks to the inner self. On the contrary, when we learn to "see" God in human interaction, we will "hear" God more clearly in moments of quiet prayer.

Writing these words, I am reminded of what I was taught about the value of various kinds of prayer. The model with which I was presented is found in the story of Jesus' visit to the home of Mary and Martha (Luke 10).

When Jesus arrived for his visit, Mary sat at his feet to listen. In the meantime, Martha rushed around and prepared a meal. If you remember this story, Martha came to Jesus and complained that Mary wasn't helping to prepare the meal. But Jesus told Martha that Mary had chosen the "good" portion and that she, Martha, spent far too much time worrying about the details.

My teachers drew the conclusion that Mary's quiet, contemplative listening was superior to Martha's activity. So contemplative prayer was far more pleasing to God. And yet the Gospel doesn't say that Jesus refused the meal or that Martha's gift was unacceptable.

Another point to ponder: when next we encounter Mary and Martha, it is at the death of Lazarus. Read carefully John 10 and note that Martha, not Mary, the contemplative one, recognizes who Jesus truly is. Martha, not Mary, proclaims Jesus as Messiah. From her work, her activity, from her own manner of reflection and prayer, she comes to understand who Jesus is and the meaning of his ministry. Does this mean her way is better? No. Martha's way is *different*. Whatever you do, do as well as you are able. Contemplative prayer is only one way of coming to experience God. God will speak within your honest searching, be it in quiet prayer or in activity.

Speaking about God

What can we say about God that will truly describe the One who called all life to be? It is easier, perhaps, to say what God is not. Still, when we speak from the heart, when we are authentically in touch with our connection to all that is living, we begin to intuit the great mystery of the Knowable, Unknowable One.

In the Jewish experience, revelation comes in the dynamic words "I AM!" So, too, whenever we are asked to reveal our identity, we also state "I am . . . ." This points to our profound connection with the very Source of life.

Listen again. You will hear that this God is not a name, not a thing, but very much a dynamic Other, the very heartbeat of this momentary pause in the Eternal Present.

Time is such a mystery. Could it be that human beings were given a past and also a future because God cannot experience them except through us? And could it be that, in order to come fully into life, we need to put aside our preoccupation with past and future and to learn to live wholly in the present? For God is only discovered there!

There appear to be three ways of speaking about God. The first and most important is the religious language of everyday people, built on very human things – loving, birth, death, success and failure, to name just a few. This is the way of all deeply felt human encounters with God. This allows every man and woman to know what it means to be alive, what it means to hope and dream, what it means to be human.

Another way to speak of God is found in the language of theology. This formal, "professional" language is rooted in the language of everyday experience and cannot be understood without it. In fact, theology can be irrelevant if it is not rooted in simple human intercourse – the lifeblood of human existence.

A third way comes from the shared life of mystics, who encounter God directly while contemplating and being in touch with the world. Unfortunately, much of what these women and men expressed was dismissed and held suspect because it did not fit the categories of classical theology.

All these ways of speaking about God are valid. All can have a part in leading us to God and to the expression of who God is. None is better; all are unique and all are essential, given the range and variety of human creation. Why would we deny any one way or any one path that leads us to God?

We need to be wary of defining God for others. Our primary task is to encourage all persons to formulate their own image of God based on their encounters with the Creative Source of life.

I am reminded of an occasion when I was asked to address an inter-faith gathering of religious educators on this very topic. I was puzzled and intrigued by the challenge of meeting all their needs.

This was a unique group, coming together from more than ten denominations, with very specific traditions. I knew little of their personal faith and little of their personal vision of God. Who was God for them? What did they believe about God's self-revelation in Jesus?

On an impulse (inspiration?), I gave each of them a blank piece of paper and asked them to draw their image of God – the one they presented to their students. They happily took to the task. However, after a few minutes, the room was filled with an intense silence. When the silence became uncomfortable, murmurs arose and people looked at me strangely. Finally, one woman stood up. She was upset and stated that I had given them an impossible task. There was a chorus of agreement and then silence again.

I asked them to consider that they had been "drawing" God for others for years. Again silence. Then we began to work together in order to determine how to lead children to discovering God in their daily life and experience. I think all of us were challenged and changed that day.

Through the grace of this experience, I came to see that we have been a little too glib in defining God, the ultimately indefinable. This, of course, need not make what we do "wrong"; rather, it illustrates the care that we ought to take. God can be obscured by the limitations of the images we use.

The Hebrew and Christian Scriptures sum up the Jewish and Christian experiences of God, but the scriptural language is not divine and need not bind us to rigid patterns in thinking or in praying. Scripture arises from a people's struggle to define the meaning of their relationship to God, with one another and with the world.

When we write or speak, we must ensure that our words don't block an encounter with God. The language of theology is no exception. Theology is institutional. Far too often, its specialized language is understood only by professionals. But speaking of God belongs to each person and needs to be expressed in the language of the day.

Let me give you an example: after the birth of my first child, I was deeply moved by his impact on my life. Each night, I would tuck him in and stare in awe at this marvellous spark of life. One evening, I was drawn to touch him and pray. As my hand caressed his forehead, I was, for one instant, "turned inside out." This is the only way I can describe what happened. I "knew" at that moment — as surely as I know my very own name — just how God feels about each of us.

I stood as a father before my own child and knew God as *my* Father.

A Parable

Once there were two friends — Man on the Left and Man on the Right. They had their differences, but shared many things in common. One thing they both loved to do was to visit Man Who Had No Name.

Through the years, they grew to treasure their visits to Man With No Name. They talked one day about what they would like to give him in return. They observed that he was different. He did not have the same compact features which they both possessed. And so they decided to give him their own "look" — a look they thought of as beautiful.

Each night for a week, while the Nameless Man slept, they changed one of his features. They could hardly wait until the work was done and the Nameless Man would notice. However, on the morning of the seventh day, after completing all the changes, they discovered that Man With No Name had died.

Moral: Let God be God!

(Based on a parable
from the works of Chuang-tzu)

A Story about Words

Words are sacred!
Words are living!
They have the power to name what is true and real. Words are keys to open and close the doors to life. They can hurt or heal, free or imprison, and even cause life and death.

The words we speak can be stepping-stones or traps!

They become traps when they limit the exploration of life, denying any part of it; stepping-stones, when we use them to reach beyond where we now are and what we experience.

When we speak too often, too long or without care, our words become an avalanche, blocking the path that we and others walk. They cut us off from where we seek to go. We lose the sense of their sacredness and their power when we multiply them unnecessarily.

And . . .

. . . it was from the First Words that all we are, and all we can be, was first set in motion.

Beyond the here and now, before time and space came to be, there were Three. Together they shared what we now seek. Out of their sharing came three words:

"I Love You!"

And their words were of a kind that could not be contained, and as they spilled forth:

"I" reached out and fired the stars which hang in the immense darkness of creation.

"Love" forged the earth and filled the hollow places with the waters, that the stars might be reflected.

"You" brought forth all living things — crawling, flying and swimming things — that the skies, the earth and the waters might live creatively.

But as the Three looked upon their gifts to one another, they felt words not fully expressed. Together they called to life another — like, yet unlike, themselves. Woman and Man, two halves of a whole, were created. In each, a part of their essence is carried; in both, an intimate nearness is reached.

To the man and woman, the Three gave the power of words. Like their creators, now they could name and so create. And with this power, they could also say: "I Love You!"

From these spoken words, you and I came to be.

These words will continue to be spoken by you and me, and by the whole of creation, until time and space are no more, and they return to the Ones who first spoke them.

Where Do We Find God?

The answer is paradoxical: we don't! It is God who finds us. This is part of the wonder of creation. Wherever we look, God reaches into the depths of our vision, our perception of life, offering us a multitude of opportunities to see. There is no place — be it one filled with joy, bitterness, smiles or tears — into which God cannot reach. So we must put away our preconceptions of who God is and let God speak just where we are.

All too often, we turn to God only when we cannot deal with life's difficulties and trials. But the God who claims us also rejoices when we solve the riddles of life, when we attain those goals which have so long eluded us both individually and collectively. The fulfillment we experience in accomplishing our tasks, in being good at what we do and being told so by others, is to be touched by the happiness of God. We just need to adjust our sights in order to find God in those places and on those occasions where and when we have not previously looked.

I am reminded of a time, almost thirty years ago, when God seemed to have gone from my life. It was a time of great emptiness. During one of my evening walks — now recognizable as the first steps in my journey of faith – I stopped to watch a magnificent storm forming over the lake near my home. There was great power in the lightning which tore open the skies. I could feel the waves of thunder vibrating right through me.

For some reason, which to this day I do not fully understand, I *knew* that God existed. My life took on a whole new meaning and an entirely new direction, which I have followed, though not perfectly, since that night.

Here, I think, is an appropriate place to pause and reflect on just some of the ways and some of the places we can open ourselves up to an encounter with God.

The most obvious place is in the natural world. This is a world to which we are intimately connected. Within the complexity and simplicity of living things, one finds revealed a creative will which brings forth life from death and lends hope to our deepest human longings. The cycle of life in nature reflects both the spiritual and physical dimensions of all women and men. The spiritual and physical dimensions cannot be separated. We have within us the seasons. This cycle is inevitable and cannot be refused. From birth through death, these patterns are evident. They come whether we will them or not. But how we use them is the crucial factor in finding God at the beginning, in the middle and at the end of life.

Those who are parents have already encountered the power of the Creator through the conception and birth of their children. They experience the patience and delight of God in their children's exploration of life's treasures. They come to understand forgiveness and fragility as they pick up their children, comfort and encourage them. And all parents know the pain of letting go as they send their children into life, just as God, our loving parent, lets us go as well to explore life's wondrous mysteries.

God can also be found in the world of culture and tradition – in the thoughts, words and deeds of our ancestors. Philosophy, history, art, music, technology and all serious human development reflect the search for meaning and, ultimately, for God. Many of the great debates in philosophy, theology, the natural and the social sciences, have centred on the nature of human existence, the meaning of life and who God is.

For Christians, the root experiences of the early Christians and our Jewish ancestors can be brought forward into our own awareness of God. The past can give meaning to the present. We should explore also the neglected beliefs of aboriginal peoples whose lands we exploited and whose faith we dismissed in our arrogant assumption that God speaks only to us. Today, above all, we need their awareness of the connection of God to the fullness of the natural world. I would also suggest that we walk with the patient people of the East, searching through their teaching, noticing that among all of them God speaks to the human heart.

We are a people moved by revelation. The Jews have the *Torah*, the *Talmud* and the *Writings;* Christians, the Hebrew and the Christian Testaments; Hindus, the *Vedas*, *Upanishads* and the *Bhagavad-Gita*; Muslims, the *Qu'ran;* Taoists, the writings of Lao-tzu and Chuang-tzu; and Buddhists, the Eightfold Path and the Middle Way. Each tradition reveals a specific way to live, a way of finding the meaning of life, of coming to the Source of All That Is.

I write primarily from my own rich tradition of Christian Scripture, which holds first place in my own search for God. Still, I have become aware of the many sides of revelation in my search to link Scripture to everyday matters. This cannot be done without the aid of prayer, nor can it be done by using Scripture to prove my point. That would defeat the purpose of the search.

Let us look at a few examples of the rich possibilities of Scripture – possibilities that can be cut off easily unless we are open to what God is telling us about life today.

Genesis appears to present to us two very different accounts of the creation and two very different pictures of the Creator. In the first chapter, we seem to be presented with a God who is far away, above and beyond the created world. This is the Creator, who sits in his heaven and simply commands that things will be. Things are done as he says. This is the all-powerful, transcendent God, having no need of what is created. This is the Patriarch, aloof, unreachable, the God of the boardroom who works to a timetable and a definite plan. This is the God who takes care of everything, clearly setting out the path to be followed.

But the more interesting account of the story of creation is that of the God who communicates directly with those who are the Creator's creatures. This is the God who creates Adam from the soil of the earth, giving his own breath to what he has formed. God gets dirty hands. This is intimacy! This is the God who walks in the garden in the cool of the evening, calling the man and woman and talking with them.

Which account is true? Neither? Both!

Read Genesis for yourself and you soon discover that, for the writers, God is real − touchable and deeply involved with what has been created. And yet there remains a profound awareness that this One whom we also call God is infinitely beyond our daily experience. Indeed we know that all life comes from this God: the garden, and the freedom to explore the mysteries that abound in life.

Consider, too, the story of Job. This story illustrates the great dilemma of finding meaning in suffering and evil. Job is faced with disaster after disaster. This is a tragedy for one who has centred his whole life on the belief that a benevolent God is the source of all that we find in life. Why is a good person − in this case, Job − subjected to such loss and humiliation? No doubt, he and his contemporaries expect that God will be fair −

that God will reward good and punish evil. But what we discover in the Book of Job is that God's sense of justice far outstrips human understanding. We are constantly reminded that we can never know completely who God is, or what life is intended to be. Nor can the purpose of human existence be found solely in clues from the natural world.

To explore this revelation about the hidden depths of the created world, read Job 38. There we are presented with the revelation that there is always more that can be said about God. The book is never closed!

In the Gospel account of Jesus, we are presented with a compassionate God who cannot abide humanity's loss of vision. Jesus' task is to share the vision which God has for human life. Jesus, too, must deal with the ups and downs of human existence; experience the exultation, but also rejection, without losing the sense of God-with-us. He doesn't speak in great abstractions, nor does he write great theoretical works. He is the harmony of his people, passionately living his mission, and is "like us in all things but sin."

In reading Scripture, it is vital to find the person behind the words. Hear the peace that flows from Jesus' presence; hear the anguish that comes from his rejection; hear the anger toward those who do not honour the heart of their own tradition; and feel the betrayal when he is abandoned. Those who go beyond the words will discover God between the lines.

Look especially to your own living to find God, because in this creation everything is connected. Nothing happens without some relation to your own life and the lives of your neighbours, too. Those who love God share their love. In and through others the love of God is made visible. If anyone tells you that he or she truly loves God, but fails to show this in daily living, that person is not speaking truth. That person reduces us all.

Looking for God is a life-long work. How boring it would be if we knew too easily life's full meaning. Listening is the key which opens the mystery for exploration. Listening is the "bread of life."

Faith

Faith, to put it simply, is the confidence which is placed in another – a parent, a friend, anyone with whom we share the intimacies of life, especially God. Faith is a dialogue, an exchange, which affirms the basic truth of living: we cannot stand alone if we wish to enter into the deepest meaning of what it means to be human.

The dialogue takes place at several levels: within ourselves, with those persons we encounter each day, with the physical world as we touch it and are touched by it, with the persons of God however we define them. Although faith always has a unique personal dimension, it is never a private matter. It is never an exclusive God-and-I relationship. Every authentic experience of God involves reaching out to the world around us. Because we are made in the image of God, we must reach out to others, as God reaches out to us. Without this outreach, the faith we cling to is highly suspect. Without this sharing, faith remains empty and is of benefit to no one.

Only in love, expressed in dialogue, does faith find validity. Matthew's Gospel is very explicit about the need to share all that is of value: "As often as you did it to one of these brothers and sisters of mine, you did it for me" (25:40).

Again, in John's Gospel, Jesus explains the focus of his faith in his mission statement: "I have come that they [you and I] may have life and have it in abundance" (10:10). As he shared his experience of God's revelation, so we too are called to share the wealth of our own discoveries and insights. This doesn't mean we'll always get it right or come up with *the* answer. But we will become more fully human in the sharing, and so more able to express our faith.

Each of us is to become a life-giver in his or her own unique way. This requires the using of our talents so that others may see what we believe, and also be encouraged to explore their own abilities with the same hope and confidence. Our uniqueness and variety offer us a multitude of ways for experiencing and expressing our humanity. This we need do with the eyes of God, who, looking on creation, found it "very good" (Genesis 1:31).

Let's examine this dialogue of faith in another vein!

Faith is the gift we give to one another in the day-to-day exercise of our own humanity. For the child, it may simply be the hand placed in that of the adult when the task seems overwhelming or when the way is not clear. In a sense, it's a surrender of the self to another, with the unstated understanding that "you truly care for me!" No one, not even the child, can maintain faith without the care following from this surrender. And this "giving over" does not weaken, but strengthens, the faith we have in our self and in others.

Similarly, a meaningful faith in God also requires that at times we do the same. We surrender our self because we don't have the answer to what we seek. This need not make our act of faith a blind act. Instead it becomes enlightened when built on the confidence and trust that the Other truly loves us and would do nothing in the exchange to harm us.

I am reminded of a time when I was a religious education consultant in a small school system. I went one day to visit one of our smaller institutions, a two-room structure far from the beaten path.

When I arrived, I took over the class, giving the teacher a break. The children and I spent our time reading stories, singing, playing together and just plain enjoying the change of pace. For me, this was a graced time, one of peace and joy as I shared in the uninhibited presence of the children.

We sat on the floor together, some on my knees and others placing their arms around my neck. All in all, I was surrounded by faith and trust which I could freely return. I told the children stories about life, about Jesus and this God of ours who loves us as a father.

Some time later, when I was back in my office, the morning mail brought me a most wonderful letter. It read:

Dear Basil:
The children asked me when God, our Father, was going to come back and play with them again.

You have to imagine the moment. In my mind I had done nothing special, but somehow the simple pleasures of storytelling, playing and singing allowed God to be revealed in the exchange. And my faith that God can and does work through simple human actions was strongly reaffirmed. Because of this letter, I have an even deeper appreciation of the power of faith and of what we can learn from the children we teach. I was also reminded of the words of Jesus: "Unless you receive the Kingdom of God like little children [with faith and confidence], you cannot enter it." Because of this gift from the children, given freely and without prompting, I was affirmed in what I was doing. I felt again the faith I often talked about without hearing my very own words.

The stories go on!

During my time in religious education, I was often frustrated by the political demands of the work. When this happened, I would leave my office and visit the local kindergarten. On one such occasion, I had another revelation of the grace of God through children's gifts.

Arriving at the kindergarten, I gave the teacher some time off and spent it just being with the children. This day, I told them I was unhappy and asked them to share something that would help me feel better. A tiny girl, sitting across the circle, said: "Did you forget? God loves you. You told us that!" All the children said: "Yeah!" For the next five minutes, they all took turns telling me good things to make me smile.

As I was preparing to leave that afternoon and I was thanking the children for sharing their love with me, I felt a tug at my hand. The little girl who had first spoken placed something in my hand and said: "This is for you." It was a tiny red maple leaf.

Faith for me now is, sometimes, a tiny red maple leaf.

In the Gospels, there are magnificent examples of faith. Who better to begin with than Mary, Mother of Jesus, at the wedding feast of Cana, where Jesus arrived with his followers. When I think of those rough and hardy men dipping into the wine, I don't wonder that it soon ran out.

Mary, obviously wanting the wedding to be memorable and not wanting the hosts to be embarrassed, informed Jesus of the problem.

Jesus tried to put her off, but Mary's faith would not be put aside. She simply told the wine steward to do whatever Jesus said. We all know the story. Her confidence was rewarded and the party went on.

John the Baptist had great faith, too. He preached the message of *metanoia* – of radical conversion. His ministry was one of preparation for Jesus. His faith can be heard in the words addressed to his disciples – disciples who complained of Jesus' ascendancy: "He must increase and I must decrease." John trusted the revelation given him by the Spirit. Without complaining about all that he had done, he courageously acknowledged Jesus as God's Word to the people.

And again, in one of the most delightful episodes in Luke's Gospel, we meet the Roman centurion who comes to Jesus with the request that he cure his servant. Jesus offers to go to his home – an unheard-of practice among Jews at that time. This non-Jew, and non-believer, recognizes in Jesus one who has true authority in life. He recognizes that whatever Jesus says he can do, can be done. The centurion tells Jesus that he doesn't need him to come to his home. He knows that, if Jesus says the servant will be healed, Jesus has the authority and the power to do it. Marvelling at his faith, Jesus tells all within hearing that he has encountered no greater faith in Israel. Just think of that moment! The non-believing Roman understands better than those who claim faith in God and in Jesus' ministry. The Gospel says that the servant was cured at that very moment. Is there a lesson here for those of us who also claim this faith in God, yet lack the confidence to let God be God?

Read, too, Mark's account of Jesus' encounter with the man whose son is an epileptic and whom the disciples cannot cure. Jesus expresses annoyance at his disciples' lack of faith. Here I can identify with the boy's father, who replies in anguish to Jesus' question about his own faith: "I do believe, help my unbelief." Jesus' response is to cure the boy. This experience should lead us to acknowledge that, at certain times, we are all unbelievers.

Peter, for his part, makes a leap of faith (according to Matthew 16). He expresses his acceptance of Jesus and his mission. Jesus asks the disciples, "Who do you say that I am?" and Peter answers, "You are the Christ." Jesus puts his question to the heart. Peter's insight comes from his love of Jesus, not from some intellectual premise. This is the same Peter who, in the time of crisis, three times denies knowing Jesus. Faith, it seems, must be tested in the fire of life. Any insight – Peter's included – needs a lifetime of experience to be realized fully. In other words, we don't just acquire faith all at once; it's the work of a lifetime.

And what of Jesus' own faith? John's Gospel takes us through his last prayers. In these prayers Jesus reveals that he is fully aware of the pain he must bear to fulfill his mission. Both Matthew and Luke show us a side of Jesus we don't expect. In the Garden, before the arrest, we find Jesus sweating from fear, asking God to let him off the hook. But it's a measure of his faith that he gives himself over to the Father's safekeeping, realizing that death is the inevitable consequence. This, it seems, is the price of resurrection!

Each of us needs to examine those matters of faith which motivate our relationships and allow us to progress in living more fully. No two of us operate in exactly the same way; each person's faith must be seen for the light it sheds on the mystery of living, for the hope that generates significant human actions.

Look carefully! Your starting points – your faith – are the only ones from which you will be called to bring your gift into the presence of God.

A cautionary note: there is a danger in thinking that, once you believe, everything will fit neatly into a package. This was made evident to me in April 1991. Five years earlier I had written some parables about the meaning of life and the questions that face us daily. The truth of what I had written became a self-fulfilling prophecy.

I underwent open-heart surgery to correct a congenital defect. In the process, I almost died from undetected bleeding. What was a story – one of my parables – actually became a summary of what I experienced during post-operative recovery.

Let me tell you the parable.

A Lesson in Humility

Once there was a gifted young man. All that he touched blossomed. People came from far and wide to hear him speak of life's meaning, marvelling at the wisdom of one so young.

In youthful pride, he sought the water only from the well of his own spirit to ease the thirst of others. One day, however, when opening his mouth, he was startled to find himself untouched by that of which he spoke. Reaching into the well, he found nothing. He had spent himself until he was empty of thought and word. Fear echoed in the hollow places of his spirit.

Moved by anguish, the young man searched deeper and deeper, refusing to accept or believe his emptiness. In the void, he failed to see the promise of which he had spoken so eloquently to others. He sank deeper into despair, unable to find the words of comfort he had given others and unable to feel that sense of calm which he had once shared with those who sought out his words.

It was at that time that the Three spoke, but he was unable as yet to hear Them.

Day after day he wandered through his oft-used words, struggling to find what he had so easily given away. Finally, exhausted, he heard his own questions: Why am I so empty? Why has this burden been laid on me? I have been true to my gifts.

Into the humility born of his suffering, and because he had come to meet his own poverty, the Three reached out again. Light flooded the darkness of his spirit, pushing aside the arrogance and the pride. Hope washed away his aching despair. At last he understood how foolish it was to see himself as the answer to others' needs. True speaking could come only through the sharing of suffering and joy. He knew then that the searching questions of others were a genuine gift, and that his hopeful words could be given only as a gift in return.

Turning outward, he found the measure to fill the emptiness. He heard the words "I Love You" in the murmuring of the leaves, in the words of others, in the stillness born of human suffering. He eagerly reached for the hands of the One who had come among us to share the tears and joys of all humans. His arid heart felt once again the waters of life flow from without to the depths within. At long last he knew that the gift of others' searching could never be met with pride but only with the gift of humility.

But he was not ready yet! One more step remained! What a fool! To have taken so long! To have been so blind! His newborn humility would not be denied, and so he discovered the greatest truth of all. The Creators — the Three — had waited for him. They had allowed him to come to his own emptiness, knowing full well that he could not accept the gift until this final moment.

Tears watered the soil of his spirit. With his new-found humility, he was able to let go of his former self. All that filled his life was renewed. No longer did he fear who or what he was, learning to be simply himself. No longer did he seek to reduce the mystery of human experience to answers in mere words. He came at last into the moment. On that day he was born again!

Evil and Sin

From the very beginning, human beings have refused responsibility for their actions. In the Genesis account of the Garden of Eden, Adam and Eve are free to explore the wonders of creation. They are expelled only when Adam refuses to accept responsibility for eating the fruit of the tree of Good and Evil, blaming Eve for what he did. This trend, this state of human nature, persists to this day.

What we have forgotten is that we are a unity of body and spirit, connected to one another in all that we do. We stress the *I*, ignoring our relatedness to each other. We live in an endless struggle to see who is best, who is the greatest and who is number one.

For much of the history of Christianity we have fragmented the human person. We have split ourselves into body and soul. The upshot is a dualistic notion of the person – one in which we equate the body with sin and evil, and the spirit with goodness and grace. Much of this can be traced to the writings of St. Augustine, a fourth-century theologian. Later, Aquinas and others applied the writings of Aristotle's philosophy, which split the person into body and soul, solidly entrenching the duality of the person in the principles of Christian theology.

But how is it that the body, a primary source of human experience, has become the so-called bad guy? It is the body which informs us and gives us form in this creation. As such, it is essentially good; it is the vehicle which allows us to touch and be touched.

Read Genesis 1:31. Observe carefully the essential goodness of the person – a goodness honoured in God's own words: "And God looked on all that was made and found it very good!"

This is not to deny or ignore sin. Any reflective person is conscious of it. The world in which we live is incomplete and imperfect. We only need to open our eyes to see the very real effects of sin.

Noteworthy, too, is the biblical command to forgive those who have sinned. This is not an option for the Christian. Indeed, it often puts us in conflict with our faith. The main difficulty is that we do not see forgiveness as part of the process of coming to maturity. With the short-sighted attitude that everything can be seen as right or wrong, with no room for exceptions, we ourselves can often become the "sinners." We beat up on those already wounded by sin – their sin, our sin, society's sin. In fact, we are specifically told in the Gospels that Jesus came not for those who always had it right, but for those who were sinners; not for those who feel they've got it together, but for you and me, persons with some growing to do.

That being said, however, we have to stop spending so much time worrying about falling down ourselves and, rather, be concerned that we do not come to a point where we feel that we no longer have any control in our living. If we are always afraid of making mistakes and running afoul of God, we may sin more seriously by losing chances to lift the burdens of our brothers and sisters.

Such an attitude will take us beyond judging and bring us to compassion – one of the most significant elements in the Christian faith. Compassion arises from the recognition that we all share limitations. Nothing else can bring us to the fullness of human life of which Jesus spoke!

Compassion isn't sentimentality. Life often requires some very difficult decisions. Nor is faith an instant remedy, but a source of strength to assist us in making good, clear and human choices – difficult choices in a difficult world. Life is not all negatives. It is also filled with goodness, with joyful moments and with graced occasions which make our efforts worthwhile.

And, above all, we must remember that life isn't fair! Just look at this world where a few possess more than they could ever use, while others die of want. Good people often get the short end of the stick, while the selfish seem to prosper. To this dilemma there is no simple answer. Still, I believe that those who seek the answer in the accumulation of things are not truly happy. The true measure of human fulfillment is found in an overflowing heart.

But what, then, about judgement?

Matthew's Gospel gives a graphic image of judgement before God. When we come before the Creator, Jesus tells us, we will not be asked to recite a creed or to number our personal accomplishments. We will be asked to account for our actions towards our brothers and sisters. Those of us with closets filled with clothes, while people are freezing in alleys, had better have an answer. This warning is for me, too! The true measure of our humanity is to be found in our efforts to make this world a place where every man, woman and child receives a welcome and the means to explore his or her unique human self.

If any of us is tempted to lay the blame for our failure at another's feet, we had better reread the account of the Fall in Genesis. Remember: God doesn't get angry until Adam blames the woman for his own actions.

I also believe that our tasks, yours and mine, direct us to positive, compassionate living, thereby freeing our children from some of the poor choices we have made on our journey.

A Parable about Evil

Long ago, men and women discovered the power of words. They took great joy in the power of naming. But some, in their fascination, removed themselves from the very things they had named. They built a tower, blocking out distractions that interfered with their search into the power of the words. They soon forgot the sights, sounds and feelings which they had once been so intent on understanding. They forgot to take time for themselves and for others, becoming impatient with anyone who did not think as they did.

In their tower, they could not hear the wind, nor could they see the rising or setting of the sun; they forgot about the stars which sparkled in the night sky. The sea with its moods went unnoticed. The forest and its creatures became strangers to them. Indeed, they soon became strangers to themselves. Running out of names, they sought to refashion the words of creation.

By rearranging the letters of the word live, the word evil was formed. The word took on a life of its own. The power of evil seeped from the tower into the world outside, becoming part of everyone's life.

Now our task is to undo a little of that which evil brings. We do this by speaking words of our own making. We need to remember, however, that until all creation returns to the life of the Creator, who speaks only the words of life, evil will not be remade into its original name.

And so we pray:

Lord of life,
you made all things good.
Help us to come to you
speaking only words of life,
words of compassion and love.
May all we find broken
become whole
in how we name
what we touch.

Life's Journey: A Parable

It was the time of passage from faith to Faith. Young people were sent from their homes into the forest to search for places in which they would find life's meaning. As did their mothers and fathers before them, they began the journey with hope in their hearts, barely aware of their own limitations.

Coming to the edge of the village, they observed the paths of those who had gone before them. Some paths were well-trodden, others barely visible in the immense growth of the trees.

Some, in pride, refused the paths taken by others as they set off into the unknown reaches of the forest. They hoped to find quick routes to their dreams. They plunged through the twisting maze of trees, heedless of the wonders before them, often marring the beauty offered. Most became lost, never reaching their goal.

Others, beginning with hope but fearful of getting lost, sought quick and easy routes through the tangled arms of the trees. But their steps became heavy with the fear in their hearts, and their hopes soon faded. Fear won out, directing their steps back to the starting place. There they remained for the rest of their lives, bitter and disillusioned.

A third group examined all the paths open to them. They chose the most travelled route, following its winding and twisting path until they could go no further. In gratitude for the joys of their travels, and moved by the peace of their journey's end, they built a home for themselves and their children. This new village became a haven for those who sought their dreams further down the path. And they named the village Wayside.

The final group comprised those intrigued by the mystery of the forest. Leaving known ways, they entered the heart of the mighty forest, delighting in its sounds and moods. When they stumbled and lost their way, they stopped to rest and to recall their dreams. With love and care, they explored and marked their passage, just in case others chose to go this way.

Finally, reaching the limits of their dreams, they stopped and built a village in harmony with the great trees. A home was made where children could grow and dream, and some day set out on their own journey. This village was called Haven.

Time passed.

Then one day it was the time for the passage from faith to Faith. The young people of Wayside and Haven went out to the edge of the mighty forest.

Some . . .

This parable is about us, and for all of us. How we proceed in life is a signal to our children about their possibilities, or lack of them. They look to us for encouragement and direction. We need to take care that what we offer them is hope for the journey they must take.

Support for Living

Faith, religion, mystical experience, spirituality — whatever we call the basis for our relationship with God — is a support, not a program. It lays out what we must do in order to live fully. It is as vital as the air we breathe. For much too long, we have dealt with religion as a system of rules accompanied by a series of rewards and punishments. This is to misread Scripture. This, moreover, does a great disservice to the creative energy which flows from the Source of all life.

Observe the Ten Commandments. What do we see? Certainly not a prescription for living, but a guide for men and women to meet God in freedom, a *way* of living that would direct them away from actions which inhibit humans from reaching out to God through others.

The Ten Commandments were given to the twelve tribes of Israel, who were essentially children in their actions as they strove to become a people. Why else would you need to lay down rules about not killing, not stealing, respect for parents, worship, and so on, unless God was dealing with an unruly, undisciplined people?

Think for a moment about how we raise our children. What, typically, is our first word when they begin to explore – when we want to prevent them from coming to any harm?

NO!

This doesn't mean that they are all bad; it points to their lack of experience as they test the waters of life. But as children grow and demonstrate maturity, we appeal to reason and extend their freedom so that they may do what allows them to relate within the community, so that they may do what leads to an awareness of their possibilities and their limitations.

Jesus reminded us that he had not come to change what was handed down, but to fulfill the tradition of his people. He took the commandments to their logical conclusion. The only laws that bind are the ones that free. "Love as I have loved you." Jesus no longer treats men and women as if they were children. His bid to free is reflected in the way he meets each person. With women in particular, he lifts the bonds of their second-class status. He even includes them among his followers.

With the poor and the outcast, the alienated of his day, Jesus shows their unique value as persons. He treats them as graced persons – as having something special which God seeks to communicate. Each person, rich, poor, believer or non-believer, is greeted as loved, as being in God's image.

In his teaching, Jesus offers a higher stage of spiritual awareness by summarizing the Ten Commandments into two basic commands. These become the criteria for making sound decisions about relationships and living responsibly. For Jesus, a profound sense of responsibility is the only foundation for essential human freedom.

Added to this challenge is the understanding that love is not a prohibition; it is a call to action, to creativity. Without this freedom and creativity, our actions cannot express the image of God. God created not out of necessity but out of an abundance of love.

Attending church is not the sole measure of the deeply spiritual person. Of course, it is and will continue to be a vital support for living fully. The Church exists to encourage growth in faith and spiritual living, centring us on the dialogue begun by God in creation.

The outcome of this dialogue is the dialogue that we have with one another. Indeed, the language of faith is most graphically described in the Parable of the Last Judgement (Matthew 25). "As often as you did it to one of the least of these brothers [and sisters] of mine, you did it to me."

Who and what we are must be expressed openly, lovingly and with care. Only in this way can we hope to live a deeply spiritual life; only in this way can we hope to experience a deepening understanding of who God is.

Jesus: Man of Compassion

When we look at the life of Jesus through the eyes of the Gospel writers, we see one who has authority over the whole of creation, one who is immersed in life, fully sharing the human condition. He points us to ourselves, to the nature of this world as essentially incomplete, as given into our keeping to name, to complete with individual and group talents. This was a task which he exercised with intense love and great care; one which he accomplished with a sensitivity that called each person he encountered to become, as completely as possible, what God has sought with us from the first moment of creation. There is no sense of superiority in his attitude toward those he met and loved and with whom he shared his life. In fact, there is no record of any time when he turned anyone away, even when they refused what he offered. Jesus called them to examine their own actions, leaving them with questions they must answer within themselves.

The Gospels show a person who loves rich and poor alike, reminding us that, wherever we find ourselves, we are called to see each child, woman and man as loved by the One he called Father. We are all children of God. But we must also note that, like all prophets, he took more time for the poor and disenfranchised. This was his link with the prophetic message of the Jewish people. It seems only right, then, that we too be centred in compassion.

What strikes me as I read through the Gospels is that each and every person is met on their own terms and made to feel that their response is significant. None is allowed to sit back and feel that "this is all I have to do." Jesus gives us the clear message that life is ongoing, that another challenge always lies ahead. This challenge is to growth and creativity – to become more human and so more like our God.

Let me give you a few examples of Jesus' attitude. No doubt, you can also find your own.

One of my favourite stories is that of the rich young man who came seeking Jesus, not for an answer, but for an affirmation that he had the *right* answer. His question was phrased in such a way that he would appear righteous in Jesus' eyes and in the eyes of those who heard his question. What a surprise when Jesus asked the rich young man for "one more thing"! You might ask, Why? I can only surmise that Jesus saw greater possibilities in this man.

The rich young man turns away in sadness, but Jesus does not condemn him. This particular story turns me to myself. Like the rich young man, far too often I want to be affirmed rather than challenged. I, too, want to have "the answer" to the twists and turns of life.

Another wonderful illustration of the challenge issued by Jesus is found in the story of the young woman caught in the act of adultery and brought to Jesus for judgement. Jesus doesn't condemn her, but challenges her accusers to take a hard look at themselves. As a result, the accusers are faced with their own hypocrisy. For her part, the young woman meets the judgement of her God in the challenge to "sin no more."

I love the story of Simon the Pharisee. He reminds me of myself. He tries to show off his broadmindedness to Jesus and his friends. He invites this dissident rabbi to eat with him in his own house. But during supper, a prostitute breaks in and throws herself at Jesus' feet, weeping for her sins. She recognizes Jesus as the one who forgives, who gives the grace she needs to be free.

But the "broadminded" Simon expresses shock that Jesus allows the woman to touch him. If Jesus is of God, doesn't he recognize that she can't be forgiven? Jesus challenges his lack of understanding. He is reminded that God has repeatedly forgiven the Jewish people whenever they too turned away from their sins.

There is one story which puzzled me for years. At the pool of Bethsaida, Jesus walks past the sick and suffering until he comes to one man. Why? In this case, the message comes not from Jesus but from the lips of the cripple. When Jesus asks if he would like to be cured, the cripple answers that he has *"no one"* to help him into the pool. This is the reason for the miracle. Jesus heals the cripple, but after he does so, he requires that the man do one more thing: give up the despair that cripples him. We learn here that to be truly healed, to be truly complete, we must live in hope.

Jesus' encounter with Pilate also stands out. Pilate threatens Jesus with terrible consequences unless he answers his questions. Jesus challenges Pilate's understanding by pointing to the ultimate meaning of authority, and leaves him to find what he must for himself. Although Pilate fails to grasp what he is told, I'm sure that Jesus' words of forgiveness from the cross also included him. It is interesting to note that Pilate considered a saint in some of the martyrologies of the Eastern churches.

Jesus, of course, doesn't just challenge others; he is challenged himself. God requires of him the same faith and trust that he calls forth in others. As the Gospels bring us to the close of Jesus' earthly existence, we find him in the Garden of Gethsemane, alone and in trouble.

He knows that the authorities are against him. He has challenged their reading of God's will, their misunderstanding of the covenant and of the message of the prophets. Although his disciples are sleeping nearby, he finds himself alone and afraid. In fact, he asks God to let him off the hook. But there is no escape, even for Jesus. God requires one more thing of his Son as well.

On the cross, we find Jesus emptied of his faith, unable to pierce the distance between himself and his Father. He cries out: "My God, my God, why have you forsaken me?" In the last moments of a life of love and compassion, he must face the greatest human pain — despair. Still, his trust in God will not be overcome, and finally he accepts his lot. His last words are his vindication: "It is accomplished!"

When we respond to Jesus with the eyes of faith, we meet the man of compassion. He is sent not only to speak about God, but to show me how to be the person I am truly called to be — fully human and fully alive.

God Speaks

Christians are taught that Jesus is the Word of God, that God has spoken from the beginning of creation, and that God is found in and through everything that is of this world, even in sin and suffering. God is the great I AM – two words that are really one – understandable only in the resonance of the human spirit. Often, however, we do not hear what God is saying. The hearing we need to develop requires all our faculties and senses – intuition, feeling, reason, and so on . . . .

What is God saying? I believe that there is a unique message for each of us to discover as we open ourselves up to God's presence in, around and through ourselves. Only you can say what is given to you; only you can share the unique revelation given to the world through you. Listen to the following voices as they share their experience of God speaking; listen to the affirmation of your own self in the shared experiences.

Demetria Martinez, in the National Catholic Reporter, November 30, 1990, wrote: "I believe that when we were conceived, God whispered a 'word' to each one of us, and it is our life's task to discover this special word, to embody it fully in our living before we die."

From the prophets, the two following quotations are read to us as children. For some reason, we adults appear to have forgotten them:

Before I formed you in the womb,
I knew you;
Before you came to birth,
I consecrated you;
I am sending you as my voice
to the people.
(Jeremiah 1:5)

Now says the Lord,
the One who created you . . .
the One who formed you . . .
I have called you by name,
you are mine.
(Isaiah 43:1)

These most beautiful expressions, once grasped, can encourage us to say back to God:

I thank You, most gracious One,
for the special word you speak to me.
You have known me from before
my mother conceived me in her womb.
You called me to life,
giving me a name,
whispering a unique word of life
that I might bring to all creation.
I go now, seeking that word;
I call you Lord
for you are also mine.

It is my firm conviction, because of who I am and what I have encountered, that God speaks to us in the birth of each new day, in silence and noise, in the first smile we meet in the morning, in the first tear we dry with compassion. Life is a liturgy in which we are called to participate. And we might ask: What is there in the chaos and violence of life which speaks of God? In faith, we can turn the energy of chaos into creativity, and the pain of violence will be met with the healing act of touching.

I dare to speak for God in the following words:

Learn from
the face of loneliness
the voice of a child
the joy of discovery
the peace of solitude
the happiness of friends
the sorrow of loss
the tedium of repeated duty
the new day
this hour
each moment
that I AM with you
reaching out
calling you
reminding you of my love.

Death

Far too often, we think of death as a radical interruption, an obscenity to be avoided at all costs. We fail to honour aging and the movement of life to its natural conclusion. This suggests that we have removed ourselves from the natural world of which we are an intimate part. In nature we are continually reminded of the cycle of life and death. All life is the inevitable movement from birth to death; all beginnings come to an end. To fear death, as many of us do, may rob us of the truly magnificent moments and wonders of living.

This is not to say that we shouldn't mourn the death of a loved one. This will always leave us a little sad. But we should remember that the loss we suffer and the tears we shed are the result of having experienced love from those who have died. We can't miss someone unless that person has made a positive difference to our lives.

Twenty years ago, my Uncle Francis died. I was halfway around the world and I couldn't get back. I didn't have a chance to say goodbye. I loved Francis as deeply as any son could love his father. With Francis, I felt peaceful and loved just for who I was. He never said much, but this quiet man spoke volumes to me.

His passing brought forth a poem. I simply call it "Francis":

Lord,
someone I loved died today
and there's this great empty spot in my heart.
I need you to fill it, to assure me that
I will see my friend again
in the kingdom you promised.
Help me to shed honest tears, but also to remember
all that was good between us.
Help me to honour
the memory of this relationship
by sharing my love with others
even as his love was shared with me.

Just a week before writing this part of the text, I received word of the death of another old friend. His name is Michael Peterkin. He was eighty-three years old, a wise, loving and energetic man. Michael wasn't perfect, and he was never afraid to express his love and his need for love from others.

When the news reached me about Michael's death, I was deeply moved. Here again, I had no chance to say goodbye. That evening, I sat outside and thought about what he had meant in my life. Strangely enough, the sadness did not last. I could hear his hearty laugh as he had greeted me each time we met. He always asked: "Did you miss me? Do you love me?" As I sat in the stillness, I thought of Michael entering into God's presence. I could hear him laughing and asking God: "Did you miss me? Do you love me?"

A deep peace filled me, and at that very moment there was a break in the evening cloud. I saw a bright star spilling out its light. I thanked God for the gift of Michael's friendship and I let him go in peace.

To Michael, I now say this:

Thank you
for your time and love,
for your compassion and joy,
for your laughter
and your searching spirit.
They are treasures
which I will hold in my heart
until we meet again
in God's love.

Death and Life are two sides of the same coin. I was reminded of this by one of my students, Natasha Nunes, who shared with me a very moving experience in the completion of one of her assignments this past spring.

In my World Religions course, students were asked, "What is the meaning of life?" They were not allowed to write a definition, since definitions often obscure the truth. Instead they were to write a poem or parable or share an experience.

Natasha's father had died two months earlier, after a long struggle with cancer. She was only sixteen, but as you can see, her response shows an understanding far beyond her years. And if you had been present at the farewell, you would have felt the love that was his legacy.

This is her response to the assignment:

The Meaning of Life!

One day a girl was sitting by her father's grave, wondering about the meaning of life. She thought back to when she was younger and saw her dad playing soccer with her. Then she saw him as he sat with her, helping with an assignment for school. Finally, the girl remembered the last time she had seen him: he was lying helpless in a hospital bed.

As she got up to leave, she looked back at her father's grave and felt his presence. With tears running down her face, she smiled, for she knew the meaning of life.

Seeing Beyond Words

In the Gospel of John, one of the most frequently used words, especially in the early chapters, is "seeing." It appears to have been chosen to help us develop an understanding of Jesus that looks beyond the explicit meaning of what he does. Its focus is not so much on Jesus' actions as on the experience of the disciples who come to see Jesus as the One who brought meaning to the community from which and for which this Gospel was written.

Jesus of Nazareth, a movie produced by Franco Zeffirelli, offers us his gospel and his way of seeing the life and actions of Jesus. The four Gospels are woven into the telling, but Zeffirelli relies most heavily on the underlying enlightenment which flows through the Gospel of John. Interestingly, however, the movie reflects also the faith and understanding of a twentieth-century man. Does this personal response diminish the accuracy or authenticity of the Gospels? No! For God continues to reveal his message within each person's experience, including Zeffirelli's. The message is revealed through our individual search into the meaning of birth, life and death.

Let me focus on just a few encounters in which Jesus asks those around him to move beyond what is visible to the eye and to find the deeper meaning which lies at the root of all he does.

One day on his way into the temple, Jesus encounters a blind beggar. He sends his followers to bring the beggar to be healed (John 9). Zeffirelli has Peter ask Jesus why he does this, since the man seems to be coping and has been blind since birth. Jesus replies simply: "He lives in darkness." One can see this allegorically in terms of Jesus' parable of the seed. In Zeffirelli's film, Jesus takes the metaphor of the seed and makes it live in the experience of healing. The darkness represents the womb of the earth. The seed struggles to break into the light, in keeping with its very nature. Its life is to be shared in and with the world. Like the seed, the blind man must come out of the darkness into the light of life. By doing this, the beggar will not only stand in the light, but will also shed light on who Jesus is, and on what he has come to share with all people.

This metaphor applies to us all without exception: we are to come into the light and to see in new ways what God would have of us, and for us. It is in this world that we are to become who we are – to fulfill what was given from the very beginning of the creative act. This is not something easily grasped with our minds alone; we must go beyond the word and the visible world and see it come to life in previously hidden aspects of our daily lives.

In *Jesus of Nazareth* we have a new vision that goes far beyond that accepted by Jesus' people. His vision challenged the very heart of the religious teaching of his day. Jesus doesn't reveal a righteous God who deals out reward and punishment from above, nor does he reveal the sort of God who belongs exclusively to any one group. Through Jesus, God opens us up to a new level of consciousness. In him are realized the statements "The

Father and I are One" and "Be perfect [that is, fully human] even as your Father is perfect." In other words, be open – like Jesus – to becoming one with the Father, to becoming fully who you are called to be. But note here that "becoming" means a *process*. We never have it made! Life is a progression; the pursuit of perfection is not to be found in a static state of being. This progression or journey, no doubt, will always entail great joy and suffering as we learn to let go and be open to the consequences of our decisions.

The one who can see only with her eyes or only with her reason is one who lives in self-defeating poverty. And this is not the poverty of the beatitudes. "Poor in spirit" is a way of seeing with the heart – with compassion, the source of our humanity. Looking at the world as we find it today, we still have a long way to go. The vision that will free us of greed, violence and fear of death, the vision of our hearts that will enable that leap into creativity and a full life, is there for the taking only when we remove our self-imposed limits.

Nicodemus (John 3) offers us insight into the struggle to see beyond conventional human categories. He is open to Jesus, yet he lives in his head. "Unless a man is born again of water and the spirit, he cannot enter the Kingdom of God." With these words, Jesus challenges Nicodemus to look beyond what he knows by reason, to search with his heart into the very words of Scripture by which he lives.

How can a person be born again? Nicodemus reasons that no one can return to the womb, but Jesus points out that all life is a becoming. There is no one way to grasp, finally and for good, what God has planned. It is beyond words or human designs. And again, Jesus calls Nicodemus to this beyond: "The Kingdom of God is among you." What a twist for the mind of Nicodemus! The wisdom of the day was that, when the Messiah came, he would establish a free people, without masters – free to worship and to live in peace. But Jesus says that the Kingdom is not something that will come only in the future, but it is present in the here and now. Search for the Kingdom now and be born again.

All earthly life comes from dying, from that which gives up its being to be born again. From the darkness and decay of the earth, flowers bloom. For a seed to germinate, it must let go of what it is to become a flower or, even food on our table. The rebirth of which Jesus speaks comes when we let go of our precious understandings, our preconceived ideas of what life is. Only then are we truly open to God and to signs of God in life all around us.

This "letting go" is really coming to *see*. It is opening up to the One who is Life and Love, who has called me to share in both. The *why* of my life will always remain a mystery, not ever to be fully understood, but to be appreciated ever more fully in the living out of what I encounter. But it will require that we take on the task of the inner journey. This is the requirement for attaining both the wisdom and the power to establish the unbreakable connection between self, other and the Source of all Life.

Here and now! This is eternity. Nothing, no *thing*, no concept replaces what I am now. Like the plant, I am to bloom in loving, to die continually to what is past so that every day I will be "born again." The hereafter does not belong to me. Only this is mine, this now. To see God is to be present to this moment, to each moment, to be born, to die, to be always where, who and what I am at this moment. And the great joy of this new way of experiencing self and God opens us up to the creative possibilities of the power within. Life, because of this awareness, becomes a great adventure – not something merely to be endured.

If we remain security-minded, we will not be open to this great adventure. We must dare to be open and to share ourselves with others. Opening ourselves up often means challenging "orthodox" ways of relating with God. The honest struggle of young people who find emptiness in our forms of worship does not come from bad faith. And the same is true of adults who find no energy in their faith community. This comes from a deeply felt need to put meaning into the acts which we designate as speaking to and with God.

If we truly care for those who share life with us, we will look again at how we express our faith. We will open our hearts to hear God speaking in ever new ways. Ritual and liturgy are both essential to the human soul. But both must change, even as we must, expressing in their forms and attitudes those things and experiences which fill life with meaning. If they do not, they will be abandoned, and we will leave our children without the threads they need to become the deeply spiritual, creative persons they are intended to be.

We are always presented with another chance to make what we do a deeper way of celebrating the presence of God among us. Openness to new ways of seeing offers hope for the life of our planet.

Another name for this spiritual vision of life is compassion, the womb of all that is truly human. When compassion is expressed in all the avenues of living, we truly come to see the meaning of the words "Unless a man be born again . . . he cannot enter the Kingdom of God." Let us all make our prayer, as we embark on this most sacred and blessed of journeys: "Lord, that I may see."

Prophecy

In the midst of all great religious searching and truth, one finds the prophet. She or he is the vehicle through which God communicates with the human family. Prophets are women and men who remind us of God's commitment to human life in all its forms.

What is it which distinguishes the prophet? It is the response to God, the God who speaks into creation about the meaning and connection of life to its source. The prophet is a voice, called to remind others of their loss of vision, their breaking of the covenant that binds all living things.

Prophets are not always well-received. In fact, God sometimes chooses the most unlikely characters to speak to the issues of life. I think here of Jeremiah. When he was given the unpleasant task of correcting his own people, he rebelled and even cursed the day he was born. Jeremiah was a recluse who did not enjoy speaking out. He was well aware of how those around him would respond to his message, and he didn't need the aggravation. God, however, works in surprising ways. He chooses whomever he desires at the time. Equally surprising was God's choice of Amos. A simple farmer,

Amos was sent to the courts of Israel to lecture the rich on their neglect of the poor.

Prophecy, then, is not the work of the specialist. No matter how highly or lowly a person is considered to be, each one is called to communicate the message in his or her own life. The message, put simply, is: "God cares about all life."

Indeed, each one of us shares in the revelation of the living God. Whenever any one of us forgets who we are or why we exist, another is called to point to the essential dignity of the human vocation. No one is free of this responsibility.

Prophetic literature is filled with lessons of great beauty which prophets have been compelled to share with us. Micah, for example, tells us that living the covenant with God requires no complex doctrine. "He has shown you, ... what is good and what it is the Lord requires of you. It is only this: to treat one another with justice, to love with kindness, and to walk humbly in the presence of God."

What a marvellous and freeing way to live! But this way of life is not easily attained if we continue to hold on to things for security. Micah's message, the Word of God, calls for discipline and a change of heart.

The prophetic message of our Hebrew ancestors is applicable today. Ours is a generation that has lost the essence of living, using religion to justify selfish and wasteful lifestyles while the poor remain neglected. What we proclaim by creeds and by our attendance at church must translate into compassion for those around us — especially for those who have no one to care for them, who live without love and faith.

Jesus took Micah's message one "giant step" further. If you come to the altar and you find that someone has anything *against you*, you must leave your gift at the altar and first be reconciled with that person before presenting yourself or your offerings to God. Perhaps our churches ought to remain empty until we, too, are reconciled to each other.

Each must ask the question: What is my call? What word does God require me to speak? No one can tell anyone else what God seeks from a particular individual, or how the word comes into our hearts. Each of us is required to share our talents in our own community. Most of us are not required to preach from the rooftops, but only under the rooftops where we spend our time. God does not require more than we can give. Besides, if we all were on the rooftops preaching the message, there would be no one left in the streets to hear.

Conscience

Conscience is that inner faculty which separates us from all other species of animals. Conscience is the capacity of the human spirit to examine its experiences and attitudes from a moral point of view. That capacity is, however, no guarantee that we will always do so correctly. The pain, evil and suffering in this world give bold testimony to just how underdeveloped this capacity can be.

In some ways, Shakespeare was right: conscience does make cowards of us all. In moments of decision, we are often left to our own devices. Often we make the "right" decision based on how we will look, or how we can make the situation better for ourselves. But informed conscience and consciousness compel us to be aware that regard for others is the decisive component of good solid decision. In this we are like our Creator Lord.

In most of the things we do, we have a sense of what is good and right. The difficulties arise in assessing the consequences of moral choices and how they will affect those around us.

Conscience is supreme! Whatever we encounter is to be set against this God-given gift. When we come to the final moment or, as some might put it, when we stand before God's judgement, this will be the measure of our eternity.

The churches have taught this basic understanding of the relationship between the conscience and life experience for centuries. But how often do we hear the supremacy of conscience preached or stressed today? Some church leaders want to tell us what is best for us. They want conformity and they want to control. But conformity is a reduction of human potential and a gross misunderstanding of the uniqueness that God has imprinted on creation. The rigidity which denies the creativity of God is a sad commentary on the development of faith in the human spirit.

What will we say to this God, in whose name we claim to speak, about our intolerance or our inattention to those people on whom we sit in judgement? If our mission is to declare a loving God, then we have failed miserably. If many can't accept what we say, it may be that we just have not grasped the meaning of the Word ourselves; perhaps, too, we have not been open to hearing God speak through *all* created life.

We all know that empires spread across the world under the guise of the Christian religion and that the human rights of many peoples were seriously suppressed and violated. Instead of establishing common threads to share and nurture belief, we forced our ways on other peoples. We impoverished them and ourselves by setting up social patterns that segregated persons by colour, belief and wealth.

If conscience is the rule of faith and the measure of finding meaning in human existence, then the atheist, the animist and also the agnostic deserve our respect in their search for meaning. I am not suggesting that we should leave people in ignorance, or let those around us wander or drift aimlessly until they find truth for themselves. We are called to invite others, through our words and actions, to explore what we, too, have to offer and what we believe God has offered through us.

If I were a betting man, I would wager that many of those who do not know God will more easily find a home with God the Creator than those of us who claim to know God and God's will for ourselves and other peoples.

The challenge is to relinquish a grasping for security through moral righteousness by opening up to the mystery of God. This is the ground of a refined conscience and the true mission of the human person. It is the sort of journey we cannot make alone. Nor can we make it in arrogance.

A Parable about Leadership and Service

I would suppose by now that you suspect I'm a bit of an anarchist – an anti-authoritarian person. In this you are correct. Life has taught me that those who are given authority all too often forget why they have it and where they got it. I think most of us feel deeply that one is given authority in trust and that trust, in turn, must be honoured with acts of service. The following parable illustrates how I feel about this issue.

There were once two kings whose lands bordered on a magnificent river valley. The valley climbed into mountains on both sides, from which the waters of the river flowed. Like all men, each king had a need to serve and to be loved by those he ruled. Both tried to do the best for their people.

The first king was named Drum, after the immense kettledrum with which he announced to his people what he wanted of them. Drum loved everything in its proper place, and during his reign, all were required to march to the beat of his great drum. He feared that, if they stepped to other rhythms, they would break the flow of life and bring havoc into the kingdom.

Not very long into his reign, he noticed that many people drifted away from his kingdom. There was not much laughter or happiness in the land. In fact, death was a too-frequent visitor, and the numbers of his subjects soon grew thin. Being a good man, the king was deeply disturbed in his heart because he truly did not know what was wrong.

After much thought, he set out to seek the counsel of his friend King Chime, who ruled the kingdom across the river valley. Chime got his name for the great bell which sang out and echoed off the mountains when he wished to share news with his people.

Chime loved his people and encouraged them to make bells of their own, all with different sounds, so they might join in the music of the kingdom. And in the making, new melodies were born each year for great events and celebrations. Chime's kingdom flourished. No one was ever lonely because of the melodies of the bells. There was much happiness in his kingdom, and death was an infrequent visitor.

As Drum marched through the mountain pass to see his friend Chime, he marvelled at the beauty and variety of the bells. Joy and peace were evident in the faces of Chime's people as they gathered to greet him with their music. It didn't take long for Drum to see that he had misread his responsibility. He spent many days listening to the wonderful melodies of the bells. He joined the beat of his great kettledrum to the melodies of Chime's people, and in his heart was born a new vision.

Immediately on his return home, Drum's kettledrum sounded its call to the far reaches of the kingdom. When all had assembled, he told his people what he had seen and heard. His next command was that all his people make their own drums.

In the next few months, the people created a wonderful variety of instruments in all shapes and sizes; they were small, medium and large, and there was even a square one. Together, Drum and his people learned to beat out many new rhythms. The booming of his kettledrum was now answered by many delightful echoes from his people. The people blossomed like flowers in a garden, and death had to wait much longer for his visits.

Once a year, to celebrate the change in the kingdom of Drum, the people journeyed across the mountains to meet the people of Chime. For three days, they mixed the beats of various drums with the voices of the bells. Many new symphonies were created in this sharing.

When Drum and Chime in turn set out on their final journey with death, the bells and drums joined in a joyful song of thanksgiving. Each king had established a time and space where those in their care could now create their own unique melody and rhythm.

Success

For far too many, success is measured by the accumulation of material goods. The myth that security is found outside oneself has forced creativity to take a back seat in our society. It is the sheer weight of *things* that is taken as the measure of "having it made." And this ultimately reduces the human potential for full expression to something measurable, apart from personal creativity. Success is measured by other people, and has little to do with self-expression or the continual inner call to find deeper and more responsive ways to live.

The desire for security can overwhelm and destroy the most beautiful relationships. I have seen the workaholic look down upon the person who isn't driven by the same desire for achievement. And I have seen people claim that their hours late at work are for the sake of loved ones, loved ones with whom they have little or no time to share.

How much money is enough? How much does it take to make a person secure? Nothing on this earth can insulate us from life's losses. Death speaks volumes about the uselessness of things. No amount of money, no number of titles, no *thing*, not even love, can prevent death. Only love allows us to move gracefully through the moments of living until we come to the next phase of our existence.

Success is not a thing. It is found in self-definition – in the freeing of the inner person. The successful person connects and balances the whole of his or her experience.

If I had to establish the boundaries of success, I'd have to say that, paradoxically, it has no boundaries at all. It, like its elusive partner, happiness, is found in the exploration of the deeper aspects of the self. It is a by-product, not an end-product, the grace of coming to know that where you are is an opening to where you have to go.

Since stories always seem to me the best way of expressing elusive concepts, I offer the following parable:

Once there was a beautiful village nestled in a natural harbour by the sea. In this village lived two men. These same two men can be found in every village throughout the world.

The first was a prosperous merchant, whose wealth came from the trading ships constantly putting into the harbour. He was a ruthless man, concerned only with profits, which he claimed were gathered for the sake of his family. He was so busy making his fortune that his wife and children became strangers to him. In time, they came to despise his hypocrisy. Even his eldest son, who was as ruthless as he, held him in contempt. No one loved this merchant.

The second man was a simple fisherman, who lived by the sea with his family. His home was modest, but rich with love and shared peace. He was a friend to both the wind and the waves, respecting them and caring for the bounty which the sea provided for the feeding of his family and his neighbours.

In the evenings, the fisherman sat with his loved ones, gazing across the expanse of water, sharing the wisdom and love he had learned from his own parents. By the light of the stars, he spoke of the great giving of the sea — the mother of all that lives. His children sailed with him and shared with him, growing daily in their love for him and for the bountiful world around them. All who knew him were touched by his gentleness and love of life.

In the home of the prosperous merchant, when evening spread her dark cloak over the earth, the miser closed himself behind the doors of his counting room. For hours he sorted the small stacks of gold and silver, loving the feel of the coins in his hands. But his face showed joy only when his money was finally tallied and safely stowed away.

Time passed swiftly. Both men entered into the evening years. But there was a great difference in what came to pass for them.

The fisherman's children took over his trade. He watched with pride as they, too, showed respect for the bounty of the sea, and for their families and neighbours. In them was the strength of gentleness which had guided his life and which they had learned at his side. The fisherman was treated with respect and love — they even listened to his ramblings with signs of deep affection.

But in the merchant's home, it was now the son who locked himself away behind the door of the counting room. The old merchant was cast aside, barely tolerated by the family for whom he had gathered his great wealth. Contempt was heaped on the old merchant because he could no longer help in the accumulation of the piles of gold and silver coins. He was alone, ignored, unable to find even the small comfort of counting the money he could no longer call his own.

When death came, the merchant cried out in anger and bitterness at the emptiness of his life. There was no one to whom he could confide his fears or from whom he could take comfort for the journey ahead.

In the old fisherman's cottage, as death beckoned, the shadows of fear and despair were absent. He had the light of his love and the love of his family and friends to serve him as a guide. It was he who turned away the clouds that bring empty tears, who left in his dying a legacy of peace and joy.

The moral to this story?

We are not what we do
or what we have.
What we do and what we have
ultimately express who we are!

Taught by the Spirit

"I" am "other," not separate!

If I truly understand this, life flows on; if I do not understand, life still flows on. Cause and effect are separate only in the speaking. The search for ever-deepening relationships is but one of the clues to this greatest of human mysteries.

When I come to realize that I am of God, I am free to do things in a loving, creative way. I am no longer bound by, but inherently part of, the flow of the universe. I can find compassion and responsibility in all that I do. I am more than I am. The separate *ego* is an illusion. The *I* is known only in knowing the other.

Now and not now!

To seek the why of creation is futile. For in God, "why" has no meaning other than "because." "Be still and know that I am God!"

We know something of death in the midst of our lives. In sleep, we die to what has been. Upon awakening, we are reborn. Born to a new day, we are called to this present moment. This is all we can ever truly possess. This, too, is our eternity.

"I am the Way, the Truth and the Life"

I am first and foremost a Christian by education and, finally, by choice. Although I have reflected on a wide range of religious beliefs, I have always come home to belief in Jesus. He points me to myself and to the meaning of my living.

The Way: I have found that the exercise of gentleness and compassion is the most effective way of living who I am.

The Truth: I am connected to all life without any sense of superiority. As often as you do it for one of my sisters and brothers, you do it for me.

The Life: I have also found that those who touch my life – to the extent that I am in God – find strength and life in their fullness. Only connectedness gives meaning to this life I call *me*. Jesus said, "He who sees me sees the Father," and, "The Father and I are one." Inasmuch as I am of the Father, these have become my words. All else is illusion.

The Second Coming

As we enter into fullness with Jesus, we have an anticipation of the Parousia – or what others have called the Second Coming. It is not simply about the end of the world!

We meet in Jesus not a God who would destroy the loving work of creation, but a God who has given into our hands the task of bringing meaning and fulfillment to all created life. Our salvation is our identity with the Act of Love and Creation which flows in, through and around us. We bow our knee not to a God who rewards and punishes, but to One who calls us, here and now, into creative life and freedom.

Love

Love spoke the self into creation, taking the nature of man, pointing to each self as spoken word, calling each to connect with the greater Self – the Three who live in Love. The call: to live in love with and within all that is.

This Jesus of whom we so glibly speak wrote no books, preached no theology, was in himself theology. In his living, dying and living again is theology – one unclouded by false understandings.

Self

In a moment of peace, I praised the Lord of creation for all that was given me. And God showed me the one thing for which I must give praise the most. It is my Self!

Nothing

I am nothing – no *thing* – simply energy in time and space. What we are is too often held back by our definitions, by the terms, of time and space. We need to let go of the definitions, and the limitations will withdraw from who we are and from who we can be. For life is no *thing* but a great *becoming*.

Shadow–Master

In the valley school of Salim, there were many teachers famous for their learning. Young men came from the far reaches of the world to sit at their feet and drink in the wisdom of their words. Among them, the teacher named Arleth was uncommon in that he would accept one student only at any given time.

In the twenty-seventh year of the Unicorn, an unusual event took place. To the valley came a thirteen-year-old maiden seeking admittance to the school. Until this time, the school had accepted only male students. The maiden, named Ria, craved knowledge and had travelled a great distance to follow her dream. In spite of scorn and ridicule, she dared to challenge the ancient precedents. Recognizing her thirst for learning, Arleth accepted her as his student apprentice. There were a few eyebrows and voices raised, but what else could be expected from someone as radical as he?

Ria felt his wisdom from the very first moment, despite the unorthodox methods with which he chose to impart his lessons. Each day brought new experiences and great joy in the exploration of the wonders and mysteries of life. Still, one action puzzled her deeply. On sunny days, Arleth would never walk beside her; he always stayed ten paces back.

At first this upset her. She almost felt rejected. Arleth, however, was always kind and gentle, answering questions or posing twists to what she asked. And so she put aside her feelings of disquiet, plunging even more deeply into her assigned tasks.

Whenever Ria called Arleth "Master," he refused to answer. He waited for her to use his name. He, in turn, never called her "student" or "mistress," but always Ria.

Other teachers were surrounded by numerous students who called them "Master." These young men looked with contempt at Arleth and his "token female." But Arleth didn't seem to mind, continuing on as always in serene good humour, enjoying all he shared with her.

On one sunny day, when Arleth, as usual, was walking ten paces back, Ria stopped suddenly in her tracks. She turned and asked Arleth three questions: "Why do you walk behind me on sunny days? Why will you not be called Master? And why do you let those around you treat you with contempt?" Arleth smiled, put his arms around her and led her to sit within the shade of a sturdy oak.

"Ria, my little earth-child! The essential lesson in life is to cast one's shadow and not to walk within another's. No one is master over another person. All persons throughout the entire journey of life are students, learning from and with one another the multitude of secrets which the universe holds.

"I am not your master! Like you, I am a pilgrim on this journey. What we share — my wisdom and your seeking — are of equal value. The shadow you cast will be the exploration of your gifts. To live life fully is to cast your own shadow well.

"As for looking down on my methods, I have learned that it is not what others think that really matters. Only those who are insecure in what they are doing look to others for affirmation."

Time passed. Now in the valley of Salim there were two unusual teachers. Each accepted only one student. Arleth chose only young women; Ria chose only young men whose lives were moved by a deep thirsting for the answers to the great questions of living. One could often see them on a sunny day walking ten paces behind their students.

The Key to Wholeness

Many wonderful Zen sayings can help us stretch and illuminate the spirit as it searches for wholeness. Here is one of those profound statements that I have found challenging for my life:

"If one loses a key in the water, one must return and go into the water to retrieve it."

This reminds me of Jesus' words to Nicodemus: "Unless one is born again of water and the spirit . . . ."

This insight points to a fundamental formula of healing, exercised in the arts of counselling and therapy: if fear is holding us back, we must return to the fear to find release. Impediments to living life fully must be confronted and honoured as part of our human experience. Each of us has challenges and issues to face as we progress in our search for spiritual fulfilment.

Let us pray for and support one another as we seek the key to deal with the movement of the Spirit within us.

Prayer and Prayers

An Introduction

Prayer can be, and is, many things! It is often an inti-mate sharing with another person, since God is present in both the one who shares and the one who listens. The reflections in this book are prayers, too, because I am sharing them with you.

At this point in my writing, I have moved from reflec-tions to a more traditional way of praying. These prayers are the foundation of my search for God and my self. I have chosen prayers that reflect the manner in which I was initiated into prayer. The first two sections express the words and hopes and struggles of our ancestors in faith. They have much to say and offer about God and life's meaning. The last group consists of prayers that I have written to express everyday concerns and experi-ences.

You can find the list of prayers and their themes in the index. Use it as the spirit moves you. There is no specific order – only a free flowing of the words which have moved me and have touched the lives of those with whom I share faith.

The Psalms have magnificent and time-travelled thoughts and feelings. You might note that I have taken the liberty of changing some words and compensated for the shift from first to third person. This is not to challenge their manner of speaking about God and life. It is an attempt to draw on concrete experiences that touch the living of all persons, both then and now. You might want to use them just as you find them in your Bible.

Please remember that these are my ways of interpreting. As you read and pray, you may find other words and phrases more suited to your way of expressing yourself. Change them to reflect your own living and they will surely endure, because they flow from your heart to God, whom our ancestors experienced as the One Who Listens!

I would also suggest that, as you pray these words, you formulate your own prayers. This is yet another step on the road of maturing, deepening spirituality. Remember: God seeks you as you search through your experiences for your true self and the meaning of your existence.

Confidence in God

(Psalm 27)

You, Lord, are my light and salvation;
what shall I fear?
When evil weighs heavily on me,
taking my strength,
it will not overcome
but shall fall away in your grace.
Hear me, Lord, when I cry out,
be gracious and answer me!
You have told us to seek your face.
My spirit cries out to you;
your face is what I seek.
Do not hide it from me.
Do not turn away from me,
you who have always been my help.
Do not forget me, Lord of my salvation!
My mother and father could not love me,
but you, Lord, have taken me up.
Teach me your ways, Lord,
that I might not give in to my fears
nor let my anxieties
crowd out your goodness.
I believe that I will see Your goodness
even in this life!
I will wait for you, Lord;
I will be strong and wait for you.

When Troubles Leave Me

(Psalm 30)
I cried out to you, Lord,
and you heard my voice
and healed me.
You have lifted me
from the depths of despair
and restored my life.

When I was in trouble
I called on you, Lord.
What profit in my despair?
Who will there be to praise you?
You have always been my helper!

You have turned my mourning
into dancing;
you have freed me from my grief
and filled me with such gladness
that my soul praises you
and cannot be silent.

I cried out to you, Lord,
and you heard my voice
and healed me.

When God Is Clearly Present

(Psalm 40)
I will tell everyone
of the good news of my deliverance.
I will not stop telling
nor hide the joy of your saving love.
I will speak of your faithfulness
and your saving ways.

I ask that you, Lord,
never withhold your love
and your mercy from me.
Let your faithfulness
ever preserve me.
For there are times
when evil separates me from you
and my own failings overtake me,
leaving me unable to find you.

Though we are needy and poor,
you are always there to help
and to deliver us
from the power of evil.

May all who seek you
rejoice and be filled with gladness;
may those who love your ways
speak out and say:
Great is the Lord!

For the Gifts of Creation

(Psalm 8)

Lord, great is your name
throughout creation!

When I look upon the heavens,
I see your hand
in the moon and the stars
you have placed there.
Ah, Lord, what are we
that you take thought for us?

You have made us like yourself,
you have filled us with your spirit,
making us masters over your works.

You have placed all things
at our feet:
animals, birds of the air,
even creatures of the deep
are given into our care.

Lord, great is your name
throughout creation!

For Troubled Moments

(Psalm 22)

My God, My God,
why can I not find you?
You seem so far away.
I call on you day and night
but I cannot hear you answer.
And yet, Lord,
you have always rescued me
when I called upon your name.
Here I am, alone, without hope,
and I am surrounded by those
who mock my faith, saying:
If your God is real, where is he?
Fool to trust in God!
And yet it was you
who brought me forth
from my mother's womb.
From birth I have called on you.
Be near me now as troubles
surround me.
I have no one but you to help.
In you I place my trust!

The Lord is My Shepherd

(Psalm 23)

You, Lord, are my shepherd;
I lack for nothing.
In meadows of green grass
you give me rest.
To waters of peace you lead me
to revive my spirit.
You guide me on the path of goodness
for the sake of your name.
Though I pass through
darkness and despair,
I will not be overcome
because you are with me,
giving me strength.
You offer the things of life
while around me others offer death.
You anoint my head
with the oil of your joy.
Ah, how my heart overflows;
how goodness and mercy
are part of my life each day.
My home is with you, Lord,
for all the days of my life.

Looking for Reassurance

(Psalm 17)

Lord, hear my call
and listen to the appeal of my heart;
lend your ears to my prayer,
the words of my longing.

You see the depths of my heart.
No sin fills me,
no words but those of faith
pass my lips.

I treasure your word.
I seek the paths you set before me,
that I might not stumble
on the way.

When I call, you have always answered.
Hear me again
and turn your face to me.
In your kindness,
bless me, your servant.

For the Surprises in Life

(Psalm 139)

I sing your praises, Lord,
for you are wondrous,
the God of surprises!
You formed me
and wove me together
in my mother's womb.
From the moment of my conception
you have known me,
even in what I was still to do.
In your book are written
all the days of my life.
I praise you,
for you are wonderful.
You are the God of surprises!

Thanksgiving

(Psalm 67)
May you, Lord, show kindness;
bless us and make your face shine on us.

Oh, Lord, show us your mercy
and bless us,
making your face shine on us!
Then all the people of the earth
will acknowledge your ways,
all the peoples will know
of your saving power.

Reveal yourself to all the nations
that they may sing with joy,
knowing of your justice
and your care for all people.

This day, the earth gives us its abundance.
You, Lord, have blessed us
and shown your kindness
in the rich bounties of your creation!

Continue to bless us, Lord;
show kindness
and
make your face shine on us!

For Strength

(Psalm 86)

Listen to my voice, Lord, and answer me
in my need and poverty;
guard my spirit as I follow your ways;
save me, you in whom I place my hope.

I call on you throughout the day,
seeking what will lead me to rejoice in you.
For it is to you, Lord,
that I lift my spirit.

You are good and forgiving,
giving love to all who call on your name.
I call you now, Lord.
Hear my prayer
and listen to the pleading of my heart.

When I am in trouble, I call on you
and you answer me;
there is no other God like you.
No one loves us as you do.

Other Scriptural Prayers

Beyond Words

(Sirach 43)

Though we speak many words
we cannot say all,
and the final end of our words is:
you are all.
Where will we find the strength
to truly praise you?
You are greater than all you have made.
Awesome are you, Lord,
and we marvel at your power.
When we praise you,
although we put forth our greatest effort,
this, too, you surpass.
When we proclaim you with our feeble efforts,
although many, still this is not enough.
Who is there who has truly seen you
and can speak to us of what you are?
Much of what you have done still lies hidden,
and we know so little of your greatness.
For you, Lord, have made all things,
and you grant wisdom
to those who come seeking you.

A Blessing

(Numbers 6)
May God who is love
bless you
and keep you!
May God who is known
in creation
show you his face!
May God who is compassion
look on you kindly
and grant you inner peace!

For Wisdom

(Sirach 9)
Lord of life, Compassionate One,
you who speak all things into life,
teach us your ways.
You have given to us,
both male and female,
the care and cultivation
of the works of your hands.
Grant us wisdom
that, serving you
in truth, justice and holiness,
we may come rejoicing
into your presence
on the final day
of our earthly journey.

Prayer for Every Day

(Psalm 95)
We will praise you
in joy each and every day,
telling of your strength
and of your constant love.
We will greet each day
singing words of thanksgiving.

For you, Lord, are great
beyond all gods.
From the earth's foundation
to the mountain peaks,
everything is yours.
The sea, too, you have made,
the land you formed
by the workings of your hands.

We bow before you,
telling all that you are our God
and we are your people
for whom you care.

Mary's Prayer

(Luke 1)
My soul mirrors your glory
and my spirit rejoices
in your loving mercy
shown through me,
your humble servant.
From this moment
all will know of your blessing
because of what you will work
through my trust in you.
Your name is holy
and you have shown again your mercy
to each generation
which honours your name.

A Blessing on God

(Nehemiah 9)
You are blessed, Lord God,
throughout every age.
All life, knowing or unknowing,
proclaims your glory.
Yet yours is a name
beyond all blessing and praise.

You who are God alone,
we bless you
for the heavens with its stars,
for the earth and all it yields,
for the seas and all life within.
You are the source of all,
and creation rightly
sings of your greatness.

God's Commission

(Micah 6)
Listen, my children.
I will explain to you again
my deepest desire.

This and only this
is what I require
of each one of you:
that you treat with
one another in justice,
that you love
one another tenderly,
that you walk with me
in humility.

In Challenging Moments

(Isaiah 43)
It is the Lord who speaks:
Do not be filled with fear,
for I have made you my own,
calling you by name.
Even if raging waters surge around you,
I will not let you drown.
Even if you must walk through fire,
I will not let it consume you.
For I am the Lord, your God,
the One who saves you.

A Blessing for Someone You Love

(Ephesians 3)
Out of God's boundless glory
may you receive the power
of the Holy Spirit,
and so grow in strength,
that Jesus may dwell
in your heart by faith,
and then, rooted in love,
may you, with all the saints,
begin to understand
the length and width,
the height and depth
of all things,
and,
coming to know the love of Jesus,
which is beyond
all human understanding,
may you be filled
with God's grace!

Jesus' Prayer

(John 15)

This is my commandment,
that you show love to one another
as I have shown love to you.
And know that there is no greater love
than the giving of one's life
for a friend.
You, too, are my friends,
if you do as I have asked of you.
I shall no longer call you servants,
for what servant knows fully the master's business?
I call you friends also
because I have shared with you
all that I have learned from the Father.
You did not choose me,
it was I who chose you
and I ask that you bear witness
to what I have accomplished.
Know then that the Father will grant
anything you ask in my name.
Again, what I ask of you
is simply that you will love one another.

To Heal Divisions Among Us

(John 17)
And Jesus prayed to his Father:
let them be one with us,
even as you and I are one,
so that all who see them
may come to believe
the message you sent me to share.
I share with them
that same intimacy you shared with me,
that they may find unity through love
even as you and I are united.
Together, may their unity
speak to the world,
telling all
that it was you who sent me,
that I love all of them
in the same way that you love me.

In Moments of Sorrow

(2 Corinthians 1)
Blessed are you, Lord God,
Father of Our Lord Jesus Christ.
You are a gentle Father,
giving us consolation
in moments of sorrow,
that we, too, might offer
this same consolation
to those we encounter in sorrow.
Remind us that, as we share
in the sufferings of others,
so we share with Jesus
and
are a part of the great promise
coming to you in resurrection.

Simeon's Prayer

(Luke 2)

Lord,
now I can go in peace
according to what you
have revealed to me.
For now I see
the working of your saving presence,
which you have given to all your people.
This light you make shine
on all creation,
that you love each one as precious
and reach into our living
so we might find fulfillment.
And so now
I give over my life
into your gracious keeping!

Significant Moments
of Prayer

A Morning Prayer

You who are light!
As I waken to the sounds of morning
and the soft opening of this day,
I ask that you would be my strong right arm
as I go about this day's tasks.
You are
the One who calls all life to fullness
and makes the sun to rise on all people.
Open me to your gracious presence,
that I might be filled
with hope and peace and love.
Teach me your ways in all that I must do,
that others may also find what they need
to be fully alive and courageous
and kind and joy-filled.
I go now into this day
with what you have given me.
May all that is accomplished
be strong and true,
pointing to the wonder of this gift
of the present moment.

An Evening Prayer

For what has been, my God,
I give you thanks.
For what still remains to do,
I praise your name.
Grant me this night
dreams which point toward you
and what I may still achieve.
I know that as I go to my rest
I waken to my dreams.
Fill them with strength,
with wonder, with calm,
that I may come to the new day
refreshed, in hope, without fear,
seeking only that
which brings life and hope and courage
into those places
where I must go.
This I ask in trust,
knowing that you have given me
all that is needed
and yet needing to ask.

In Need

I need you, Lord God,
as all living things need
air to breathe;
as the tree needs
its roots deeply set in the soil;
as all growing things need
the rising sun
to call them from the darkness
of the earth;
as the fish and the whale need
the waters of the deep;
as the stars need
the emptiness of space
to spread their light.
Open me to the fullness of life
that I might find in my need
the grace of your presence.

The Dance

You made us to dance, Lord God,
not to dwell in sadness!
This is the end to which all
sadness, sorrow and sacrifice lead,
to the freedom
of dancing with you!

Choices

Where there is no choice,
let me enter freely;
where choice exists,
let me walk with care,
that in the choosing,
pain and joy
may be shared,
and so I will come
to wisdom.

Opposites

I can only know joy
from having known sadness;
I can only know light
from having lived
in darkness;
I can only find self
when I have shed
ego;
I can only find you, Lord,
when I have lost you.

From Nature

Learn from:
the trees bending
to touch the face of the water;
the shades of blue and red and gold
painted by the rising sun;
the difference between this
and yesterday's moment,
that I am here,
reminding you once again
of my love for you.

In Moments of Desolation

You who are God,
hear the words of my heart.
Lead me to walk in love's way.
Self-hatred and loneliness
have been my way,
leading nowhere.
I seek that
which is of life's promise,
welcoming
pain and joy as companions,
the light and the darkness
as sister and brother,
alone in emptiness,
together filled with life.

When Restless

When we are restless,
it speaks of you, Lord,
of how we are like you,
the One who must create.
Tell us what we are
"still to do"!

When at Rest

We are pilgrims
in this time and space.
When we are at rest,
you speak to us
of how precious life is
and can be.
Tell us what we are
"still to be"!

The Last Day of the Week

Lord, it's Friday again
and we are looking forward
to the rest and the change of pace.
Help us to enjoy
this peace-filled and fun-filled time,
so we may return
with energy renewed
and a commitment to give
and be
the best we can give and be.
This prayer we make with confidence
and with faith in the spirit of Jesus,
our brother and friend.
Amen.

A Blessing

May God who is goodness
bless us and give us
understanding, wisdom and grace.
May God nourish us
with treasures of faith,
preserving us
in all good things.
May God keep our steps from danger,
directing us to paths
of peace and joy.
May the blessing of the Creator,
the father, lover and friend,
be with us and remain always
in our minds and hearts
as we seek to grow
in truth and grace.
Amen.

When Confused

Lord Jesus, fill me with peace,
not the passive I-don't-care variety
but your peace, the kind that lasts
even when confusion takes over.
Come, be my centre, my touchstone.
Grant me a heart filled with courage
to turn away from no one, no challenge.
I surely can't do it alone,
although I've tried far too many times.
And you'd better know
that what you require still frightens me.
But God knows I need you
now more than ever.
Listen to me, Lord,
even as You always said you would.
I've got this little spark of faith,
but I need your Spirit to fan it into flame,
consuming my fears and weakness,
firing me into a vessel
overflowing with peace,
a vessel which sustains my spirit
and from which others may also drink.

For Self-Acceptance

Lord, you know me and love me,
even when I'm not at my best.
Sometimes I don't know myself
and cannot accept my weakness
along with my strength.
Help me to take what I am –
weak, strong, loving, unloving,
sometimes filled with doubt –
and bring it all
into your loving presence,
that there I might find the courage
to accept myself as you know me;
to use your grace
to grow into the loving person
I can be.

For Faith

Help my unbelief;
help me to accept that faith
does not guarantee against doubt.
Grant me the humility
to turn to you in confidence
when my faith flutters
like the weak flame.
Send me your Spirit
to draw light from the darkness
of my doubts.
Help me to recognize your presence
especially in the good things
that come my way,
so I might use them as strength
when I cannot see you clearly.
As you did for the boy and his father,
cast out what leaves me hopeless.
Help my unbelief.

To the Spirit

Come, you who draw forth life,
and place in me a "new heart."
Direct my steps into ways
that are life-giving.
Let me see the truth
that makes me free
to love and honour
all those whom my living touches.
Lead me to peace and joy,
the kind that readily accepts
the limitations and the potential
for living fully.
Be with me as I strive
to put my gifts into service
of the kingdom.
And so, when I come to you
in the fullness of my time,
I will come to you
with heart overflowing.

Not Another Hurdle!

I finally made it! For years I've been struggling
to overcome impatience with myself and with others.
I felt like the high hurdles runner
who, after years of practising, achieves his goal
and makes a record run.
Then the coach, you, Lord, without warning,
raises the height of the hurdles
and it's back to square one.
I thought I was doing so well.
But with the new hurdles in my life,
I've messed up again.
Is it because I forgot you,
the source of my new-found confidence?
Is this the next thing I need to work at
to avoid knocking things over?

All right!

To a Patient God

Blessed are you, most gentle Lord.
You love me even when I fail,
when I turn away and fall again.
Give me the courage to start anew,
strength for the long road ahead,
and open me to listen
to the workings of your Holy Spirit.
I bless you for your patience
and for always taking me back.
I take hope from your healing presence,
and I will overcome my weakness
and find peace at last
in the love you never withdraw.
Amen.

An Advent Prayer

Lord Jesus,
you came to set us free
to become ourselves,
to change for joy.
Be with us as we turn once again
to answer the Father's challenge,
that we live in touch
with our sisters and brothers,
with all created life.
May those who see our faith
come to experience the same joy
we find in saying "yes" to you
and so have the courage
to start again with us.
We make this prayer with the confidence
your abiding presence gives.
Amen.

A Christmas Prayer

For this day of celebration,
for this day of God-with-us,
we give thanks to you, Lord God.
Help us to find
in this blessed celebration
of Jesus among us
a constant reminder
of your loving care for all people.
May we be thoughtful
in our care for one another
throughout the coming year;
may we, too, be a sign
of your continuing presence
in all the places to which we go.
We ask this blessing
in the name of the one
who came to us as brother.
We praise you for what you give us,
for your signature on the gift
we share today.

A Lenten Prayer

Blessed Spirit, you who reside
at the centre of life,
you know our hearts;
you teach us the compassion
we need
for ourselves and for others.
Show us new ways to grow in love,
that at this time
we might open ourselves to love
those who turn away
from love's working.
Place in us new hearts,
that we ourselves might never come
to turn away from love's call.
Fill us with courage,
that we might bring reconciliation
into all the places we walk.
Amen.

An Easter Prayer

Blessed are you, Lord God,
King of Creation.
Because of your goodness
we come to this Easter Day
filled with many blessings,
surrounded by the signs of your love
in the renewal of the life of spring.
Help us to discover in this newness
a spirit of adventure and compassion,
that we might ever seek new light
and so bring to the world
with which you have blessed us
fullness of life
and the realization of your kingdom
in what we do together.
We make this prayer
with joy in our hearts,
with words of praise on our lips.
We bless you
in the name of the risen Lord.
Amen.

Exercises for Body, Mind and Spirit

Introduction

While alive,
I am constantly in-formed;
when I die,
I will be un-in-formed!

Because of how we are created, we are constantly in need of being "in-formed." Just as the physical self requires exercise to maintain health, so, too, the spiritual self requires exercise to achieve the wholeness to which it is called. In the following pages, I have outlined ways of maintaining spiritual development through specific exercises which tap and help strengthen the flow available to each one of us.

Because the physical self is a composite, the exercises include ways of opening up the senses to avenues through which we are constantly in-formed. These avenues direct us to the details of our own environment, to the rich resources of the world around us – its sights and smells, its sounds and tastes, its colours and shapes.

As I have stressed throughout the text, these exercises are only a beginning. They are not definitive. You may find that some of them work whereas others don't. You will discover that, by adjusting them to your own needs, they will grow into new and more personal techniques. As you gain more confidence, the methods will help strengthen your inner self. Don't hesitate to change or challenge their effectiveness. Remember: no one way is ever sufficient for all. Each of us is unique.

Let's begin with some basic questions!

How do you relax? Is it healthy? Does it come from natural action? Does it help you to find the inner strength to carry on, to be more creative? Does it come from artificial sources – things outside yourself? Does it block or free the flow of energy available within you?

You alone know the answers. Whatever sets you free, filled with energy and enthusiasm, should be your starting point. Whatever makes you less than happy should be rejected in the face of your need to live more fully. Whatever you do, choose with care! It's your life! You have but one crack at each precious moment. And it is your task to fill this time with the potential of your inner self. This then will overflow into compassion for all life and you will be filled with the creative energy of God which we call grace.

Eight (+ One) Ways
to Develop Spiritual Health

1. Take a few moments each week, apart from regular worship, to review what you have learned about your relationship with God. How does this translate into your daily life experience?

2. Establish a routine for getting off by yourself a few minutes each day. At first simply empty yourself of all distractions. Let God's creative energy flow in and around you.

3. At least once a week, share with someone you love what you have learned and how you have grown. This can be a simple conversation over a meal or through any shared activity.

4. Look at the needs within your community and get involved in a worthwhile project. Your talents are the clues as to how you can best do this.

5. Be aware that you have an obligation to be a sign of love and compassion. Reach out to a neighbour with a smile, a handshake, a word of greeting or an offer of help. Your gesture may be the only experience of

human warmth one of these persons will receive this week.

6. Include physical exercise in your routines. In the beginning, this can be the most important step you take in growing spiritually. After all, your body is the vehicle through which you touch and are touched by life. Whatever you do to promote your physical health will enhance your emotional and spiritual well-being.

7. Read something to feed your spirit – something more than newspapers and bestsellers. There are many fine books on the spiritual life. All of us have a duty to be well informed.

8. Each evening, before going to sleep, examine the details of your day. Look first to the good that you have accomplished. Take pride in what you have done. Then, and only then, look at those actions that you would change. Resolve to improve what you can. Leave the rest to God.

+ One: Each and every day, give yourself a hug. It's not as silly as it sounds. Stop for a moment and acknowledge that God, who is the source of your life, loves you and wants you and sees you as good. God calls you to life. You are unique. No one else can fill this time and space with your goodness. You are chosen.

A Beginning for Prayer
and Meditation

Do you ever talk to yourself?

Come on, admit it! No one will come and take you away. Talking to ourselves is an important way to retain our sanity and maintain balance; it allows us to deal with the pressures of living in a complex society. As you reflect carefully, you will see that this inner dialogue helps you focus on the meaning of what you are living and on the manner in which you address the issues of sharing life with others.

Stop and think just for a moment! What have you been talking to yourself about during the last few days? These are concerns that matter most right now; these are issues you must deal with to make sense of your actions. Have you talked them over with the Source of your life?

I've often heard people say: "I just don't have time to pray." Untrue! All you have to do is to include God in your inner dialogue. This is the best place to begin.

And remember: anything that we truly value, we find time to do!

Other Places to Pray

One of the times we're most often alone is when going to and from work. Even on the bus, with our fear of others, we might as well be alone. Do you drive to work? Turn off the radio. Do you walk or ride a bike? There is no better time to pray. Whatever you do, take ten minutes a day to be by yourself. Lock the bathroom door if you have to. It doesn't really matter where you are as long as you do it.

You've got the time. So, what now? Simple! Go to those matters occupying your mind. They needn't all be negative. In fact, when you get good at meditating and being in prayer, you will rejoice more often in the good things – that sunrise which moved you, that smile or word that helped you over a rough spot. These are graced moments.

A couple of questions you might want to ask: Are these concerns drawing attention to how I might live better, or are they distractions taking me away from a more positive attitude towards living? And do I spend a great deal of time worrying about matters I can't resolve or change?

Talk things over with God. Above all, after talking, have the courtesy to be still and listen. It may take awhile, but God will speak. Be patient with yourself. Change and growth are a slow process.

Creating an Atmosphere
for Meditation

There are several ways to improve the quality of time and place in which you pray. Some of them are described below.

At Home

1. *The place:* I have a favourite chair with a footstool. However, when the mood takes me, I sit on the floor with legs crossed and arms open or I lie down flat. This varies according to how I am feeling.

2. *A candle:* I have found a candle helps me to focus and to empty myself as I prepare for meditation. It reminds me of the scriptural words: "You are light for the world."

3. *Incense:* Besides the compelling odour, incense reminds me of the movement of prayer in my life, rising to the One who is here and yet beyond here.

4. *A flower:* Focusing on a flower reminds me of the creative energy of God, who makes all that is beau-

tiful. In God's mind, I am one of the beautiful things of creation.

5. *Loose clothing:* Meditation is the freeing of the whole person. Make sure your clothing is comfortable and not restrictive.

6. *Music:* This is one of the most practical ways to establish a mood for prayer or meditation. Beautiful music can uplift and calm the busy spirit. The following are just a few that I use:

   - *Solitudes* – Dan Gibson

   - Handel's *Water Music*

   - *La Mer* – Debussy

   - *Pastoral Symphony No. 6* – Beethoven

   - *The Light of the Spirit* – Kitaro

Walking

Walking in your favourite place is not only healthy, it frees your mind. It is a quiet time in which you can observe the flow of life. No words are required. The heart beats, the lungs clear and you are filled with peace. Even this is enough at times.

I walk by the lake early to greet the rising sun or late in the evening to watch the colours change as the sun sinks below the horizon. There I feel the presence of God. I need no words, nor any other action to experience truly my self.

There are many other places conducive to meditation – a park, a path, an open field or stream. It doesn't matter as long as I step back from my usual routines to meet myself in God.

Breathing

Pay close attention to your breathing during the initial stages of meditation. Even before you focus on the content, it is recommended that for a few days you simply work at developing proper breathing habits.

When breathing deeply, concentrate on drawing air in through your nose and filling your lungs as completely as possible. But don't hyperventilate. The breath should be deep but even. Then exhale through your mouth, expelling all the air. You will note that it takes twice as long to exhale as it does to inhale.

To do this well, find a comfortable place to sit – in a chair, in the lotus position, on your bed – or lie completely flat. Place your hand on your abdomen and feel it swell as you inhale. Your chest should not expand. When exhaling, feel your stomach flatten. Note: If you are sitting when breathing, your shoulders will rise slightly on the inhale and drop gently on the exhale.

When you're starting out, simply do this exercise for about ten minutes. One way to help you focus on the breathing and forget about the time is to play some music that lasts as long as you want to spend developing this skill. This is one of the first ways to establish the inner peace that you need to meditate.

After you feel the calm and inner peace, you will look forward to this opening exercise. It will become a natural part of your preparation. Many people use this exercise at times of stress or to relieve the boredom that accompanies some tasks.

As you begin each session of meditation, take a few moments to perform this health-giving step. You will find new energy and the peace that you need to open yourself to the challenges that await you in prayer.

- Be sure to read through each of the exercises two or three times to become familiar with their flow and their direction. This will help you to retain your concentration so that you will not need to go back and read the instructions while in the middle of your meditation. However, if you become lost in the process, by all means stop and find your focus again. After several sessions, you should have no trouble in keeping your whole attention on what you are doing.

• Also note that some days the process will go more smoothly than on other days. This is natural, especially in the beginning of meditation.

Distractions

You may notice as you begin these exercises that unwanted thoughts intrude on your efforts. Don't push them away. Experience shows that this only increases their hold on your attention. Deal with them in your breathing exercises. Allow them to be vented. These are pressing matters in your life right now. So honour them and they will usually be dispelled as you prepare for meditation.

If they persist, you might apply the following technique. Acknowledge these matters as important and then put each of them in a "mental drawer," with the promise that you'll get back to them as soon as possible.

It is amazing how their importance recedes. Often these issues will disappear altogether as you develop your meditation technique. You will have the calmness and clearness of mind to see them for what they really are. Many of them are truly unimportant in the overall scheme of life.

Exercise One:
Opening Up to God

This exercise has proven effective for everyone with whom I have worked. By the way, if you're a clock-watcher, set a timer for ten minutes. Later you won't need it.

1. Find a comfortable place, a favourite chair, a cushion on the floor. Close your eyes and take three deep, even breaths. Allow your abdomen to swell slightly as you inhale. As you exhale, concentrate on letting your shoulders drop. If three breaths are not enough to relax, continue this gentle breathing until you are ready to proceed.

2. Empty your mind of all worries with each exhalation. Don't be discouraged if this takes a little time or if you can't get beyond this point for awhile. You might hand over your cares to God by saying something like "into your hands I commend my spirit."

3. Count slowly to ten, concentrating strictly on your breathing. When relaxed, you are ready for the next step.

4. Think of some phrase, a word, a prayer or an experience that makes you feel good. What does this say about your life? Look through your thoughts to hear God speaking.

5. Did you hear some answer (even from your own inner voice)? Did a new thought pop into your head? Pay attention to what is going on. God speaks from within you, too.

6. Relax again, breathing slowly several times. Speak to God about what you have felt. Pay particular attention to the feeling level of your dialogue.

7. Finish the exercise with one of your favourite prayers. Or simply sit peacefully in the quiet. This, too, is prayer!

8. End your meditation slowly. Feel with your body the deep relaxation that has taken place. Use your breathing to prepare yourself for going back to your regular tasks. Count to three slowly before opening your eyes. Don't jump up! Savour the transition.

9. Note how much calmer you feel – how prepared you are to face the rest of your day or to prepare for sleep.

I strongly suggest that you stick to this exercise until you have mastered it. Then you will be better prepared to adopt one of the others included in this book.

Exercise Two:
An Inner Journey

1. After you are sure you will not be disturbed for at least fifteen minutes, find a comfortable place to sit or lie down.

2. Light a candle, play some quiet music, anything that fosters a peaceful setting. Focus your attention on a bright object or the candle until your vision blurs or your eyes get heavy. When this happens, let your eyes close.

3. With your eyes closed, concentrate for a few minutes on breathing deeply and slowly. When you are ready to proceed, breathe in deeply and exhale three times, paying close attention to the rising and falling of your abdomen. With each breath, say quietly to yourself, "Relax now!"

4. Notice that your heart rate is slower, your breathing has become gentler and your muscles, especially in your neck and back, have relaxed. You will feel calm and peaceful.

5. Continue breathing deeply and think back to a recent experience when you felt good about yourself. Feel the happiness go through you again.

6. When ready to proceed, picture in your mind's eye a flight of stairs. Go down the stairs slowly. Concentrate on taking a deep breath with each step. (Note: some people cannot go down. If you are one of these, walk up or take an escalator. It doesn't matter as long as you get there.) Take ten steps.

7. When you reach the bottom, stop and rest, drawing strength from your inner peace. You may want to sit for awhile in the place to which you have gone. You may want to pray. It doesn't matter whether there are words or not. Often you will just enjoy the sensation of being there. Remember, God is there, too!

8. When you feel that you want to end the exercise, give yourself the following instruction: "When I count to three (breathing slowly with each number), I will open my eyes and be very relaxed, at peace and able to handle what the rest of the day brings."

9. Don't get up immediately! Sit still for a few minutes and enjoy how you are feeling.

If you don't accomplish this on the first few tries, don't be discouraged. Everything worthwhile takes a little time and effort. This is no exercise for those who want instant gratification. This is but another starting point, and you will have to travel this path for awhile to become proficient. With growing confidence, you can use this technique with the following methods of centring.

- A variation for step seven would be to see, when you have reached the fifth step, someone you love waiting at the bottom. When you arrive, that person will welcome you warmly, giving you a hug. Feel the hug with your body. Amazingly, almost everyone achieves this warmth of feeling.

Exercise Three:
Imaging

This exercise will allow you to examine how you feel and put you in touch with your emotional life. Becoming aware of your deepest feelings can help you make decisions and changes to your day. It can open you to more creative ways of living.

1. Close your eyes and breathe deeply three times, remembering the breathing technique of swelling the abdomen with each intake of breath and exhaling slowly.

2. Continue to concentrate on your breathing until you are totally relaxed. Don't be in a hurry. This will defeat the purpose of the exercise.

3. Now go walking within your inner self. This you may do by imaging a path or mountain trail – anything that allows you to travel into yourself. Take ten steps along your inner way, paying attention to how relaxed and alert you now feel.

4. When you are ready, look around and you will see a vase. The vase is yours. It has a particular shape,

colour and texture. Touch it. How does it feel? Describe it to yourself. This is one image of your inner self having a unique quality that needs no explanation.

5. Now, look into the vase. What is there? Describe it to yourself. Do you like what you see? Is the vase half full or half empty? It doesn't matter. Just look at it.

6. If you like what you have found, keep it, enjoy it. If you don't, empty the vase and put in there what you need to feel stronger and happy.

7. Concentrate on how you can use what you have found to make the tasks ahead easier and more personally rewarding.

8. Don't be in a hurry to end this inner walk. Enjoy the time and the place where you are coming to know yourself.

9. When ready, count slowly to ten. Breathe evenly and deeply. At ten, open your eyes slowly and feel the relaxation. Don't move just yet. Savour the experience. What did you like? What other images could you use in place of the vase?

Note: This exercise is valuable for changing your attitude about your day and how you can deal with it. What you have in your vase should be helpful in achieving the calm to carry on successfully with your work. If prayer seems natural to the moment, recall that God is in all deeply felt experiences. You might ask for the grace to continue positively throughout the day ahead.

Exercise Four:
Sacred Space

*The most sacred space in the world
is where you find your self.*

This exercise is to help you find that sacred inner space which is exclusively yours. This is the place to which you can go to regroup, to pray, to be at peace. No one can enter this space but you and the One who gives you life. This is not selfish! It is a means to find your own centre, your own inner strength, so you may touch fully the mystery that is your self. Here is where you will meet God, who speaks at the depth of all experiences; here you will prepare for the major events of your life, for the sharing that makes you loved and loving in this world.

1. Close you eyes. Take three slow and deep breaths. Remember your breathing techniques!

2. When you are ready, see a path stretched out before you. It may be through a wooded area, across a meadow or up a mountainside. It is your path; walk it slowly, breathing in deeply the peacefulness. Notice what you encounter along the way.

3. When you get to your fifth step, you will come to a turn in the path and see your goal in the distance. This is your sacred space. What does it look like? Take a moment to observe the details.

4. Continue walking on your inner path. As you get closer, you will see your sacred space more clearly. Why do you want to get there?

5. You have now arrived. What surprises you about this place? What makes you feel good? What gives you the sense that "this is mine"? Explore it, touch its boundaries, sit or lie down in the space.

6. Luxuriate in knowing that this is exclusively yours. Enjoy what it offers; feel it with your whole self.

7. Know that this is the place to which you can always come when you need to feel more yourself. All you need to do is remember it and how you came to it.

8. At this point, you may wish to express your joy to the One who is there with you; you may also want to talk over a troubling matter. It's your choice. Here, you initiate the topics.

9. When you feel peaceful, you will need to return to life's daily tasks and your relationships. You may not want to go back at first. But remember: you can always come back to this sacred place.

10. Start slowly back down the path you have travelled. Focus on your breathing as you go. When you have come ten paces, open your eyes and feel the deep inner peace you have achieved on this journey.

11. This is your sacred space. You can return to it any time. You might wish to give thanks to God who makes all things unique and special, especially this space.

Things to note: The place and details of your sacred space may change. You may find something new on your return. This simply lets you know that you are growing and changing – becoming more fully who you are.

Furthermore, you may want to vary your inner journey. This could involve paying more attention to what surrounds the path – trees, sunlight, pools of shade, the texture of the path itself. You might walk barefoot, feeling warmth or coolness, or you might concentrate on the smells, colours or any special sounds.

Imagination is your only limit.

Sacred Space

I have been to that place
where eternity passed into time;
where darkness and light are one;
where chaos shares life with creativity
as brother and sister.
It is the place of my self,
that otherness to which I am joined;
it is the place of the One I name God,
that Other to whom I am also joined.
Out of this darkness light flows
to guide my steps;
out of the chaos a newness moves
into my thoughts, words and deeds.
And here, at the centre of the universe,
the empty vessel is filled
with hope and with compassion;
and here, at the centre of life,
the vessel is emptied again and again
of fear and loneliness.
Creation goes on.
And I?
I am renewed!

We have much to be thankful for in life. We need only pay attention to the marvellous variety in both the world outside and the world inside ourselves.

I wish you much joy in your explorations.

Starting Points for Meditation

You may want to read something to set the tone of your meditation. The following suggestions have much to say about the searching of the human spirit.

Scripture Passages

Genesis 1-2
Job 38
Sirach 42-43
Isaiah 35
Matthew 25
John 1
John 10:10
John 17
1 Corinthians 13
Jesus' parables

Koans

The following are koans – Zen sayings intended to take the mind out of its usual way of thinking. The koans have no one answer; however, you may find in their exploration flashes of insight for your own life.

What happens to my fist when I open my hand?

If all things return to the source, to what does the source return?

I am the apple my father ate when he was ten years old.

I am my mother's mother!

Where was I the night before I was conceived?

What is the meaning of life?

Who am I?

I am nothing!

The most sacred place in the world is where I am.

Quotations

The following ideas have proven of value in the exploration of my self. They may be of help to you.

Asked about his ability to create from stone, Michelangelo replied that he did not create form but, using his talent, released what was already there.

I am!
What I do does not make me who I am.
I simply am!
And what I am is expressed in what I do.

To be a whole person is to use one's talents in order to allow the inner spirit free access to the outer world. This is essential because the true spirit seeks to assist others in their search for freedom.

A person who allows his or her thoughts to become a source of torment is like a person freely holding a hand over a flame.

A spiritual person finds the self connected to the Spirit, which is invested in all the things of creation.

When you do not understand, you are at the starting point.

163

A Final Word

As I came to the end of this writing, I began to wonder about you, the reader, and your reaction to what these pages contain. I hope you have appreciated that I was not trying to tell you what to believe or how you should approach the questions and directions of your life. This would have been a great mistake and of benefit to no one. The question which strikes me as I put the finishing touches to this work is: "As you read this text, did it assist you in discovering greater depths within yourself? Did it open up possibilities for reaching out to the One we call God?"

For me, the writing of this book was an act of love and another starting point in my life. As I explored my own thoughts and feelings, I discovered that I still have much more to do. This awareness comes not as a demand imposed from without; rather, it flows from the exploration I have made within myself.

Much of what I have written here I have shared with my students, with friends and acquaintances. They have helped me clarify directions, ideas and feelings, and I have been led to continue my own search, to explore many more human issues as I proceed into the latter years of my life. I am hopeful that this will make me more open to the wisdom which informs all life.

Although I cannot guarantee to answer every letter, I would like to hear from you. I would like somehow to share your journey, your searching into the depths of yourself. If you wish, you may write to me, in care of the editorial offices of Novalis, and I will try to respond to your questions, your concerns and your insights.

I am a teacher by talent and by choice. I have a need to share and to participate in the growing and learning of others; I have a need to grow myself, and this need has not diminished with the years. Even before I finished putting the final touches to this book, I had begun another. I will continue to walk this path I have taken and to share what I can name.

The new text I am writing is entitled *Within the Light Given*. Some of the topics I am exploring are: mysticism, enlightenment, blame and guilt, the one God, how God exists. These writings will also include parables, prayers and reflections. The form and shape of the next manuscript will attempt to take into account the reaction I receive from friends and from you, my readers.

I want to thank you for allowing me to share what I have written in these pages. Without you, without your listening to the Spirit of Life, I would have no chance to refine, develop and express the talents given into my keeping.

Before you put this book on your shelf and continue your own journey along the spiritual path, I suggest that you go back to the beginning of the text and read again the initial parable of the pilgrim and the holy man. Look into the quiet waters of your own searching and see the unique and blessed person whom God has chosen to create. Centre your vision in this deep awareness as you seek to live fully who you are.

May the One we name God bless you and fill your inner spirit with all the good things of Creation.